PERSONAL MEMORIES OF DAGENHAM VILLAGE 1920 ONWARD

After the First World War, the London County Council began to compulsorily purchase the main farmland from around Dagenham Village to build new housing estates for the London 'overspill'.

Within a few years, the character of the quiet little rural village was being dramatically altered by the influx of thousands of new inhabitants. In the early 1960s what remained of the old village was demolished to make way for a new centre more appropriate to the large industrial town which had sprung up around it.

Jack West was born in Dagenham in 1910, and records his memories of the close-knit community and a way of life which has disappeared forever.

By the same author:
Jack West Funeral Director

PERSONAL MEMORIES OF DAGENHAM VILLAGE 1920 ONWARD

Jack West

ARTHUR H. STOCKWELL LTD.
Elms Court   Ilfracombe   Devon
Established 1898

ISBN 0 7223 2725-0

Printed in Great Britain by
Arthur H. Stockwell Ltd.
Elms Court   Ilfracombe
Devon

CONTENTS

LIST OF ILLUSTRATIONS

PREFACE

Since writing and publishing my own biography in 1988, many folk have implored me to record my memories of the quiet little Dagenham Village of which I was born in 1910, and lived through all that enabled it to grow into a large industrial town.

I have mainly relied upon my own memories and experiences. If inadvertently a small error should appear, I would apologise and remain corrected.

For readers who are able to share my memories I trust they will enjoy the book and for the many that never knew Dagenham as a village, I am sure it will reveal something of historic interest.

I would again thank Daphne for her help and encouragement to produce such a book; also my very old friends Alf Townsend, and Hilda Patten (née Reace), who have shared my interest to record something of the village life we have lived through. For the willing response in obtaining the loan of certain old photographs from the libraries of both Dagenham and Hornchurch. To Sue and Jacqui for typing the script, and my publishers for their keen ability to produce a book so collectively recording the momentous change in Dagenham's history.

Jack West

FOREWORD

Why did the village completely disappear?

Within two years of the finish of the First World War, the LCC were faced with the return of men back from the Forces demanding a country fit for heroes to live in, and rightly so. It was with the help and financial assistance of the Government that the LCC were able to launch their dramatic and panic-stricken scheme to compulsorily purchase the main farmland from Dagenham village. Their main object in mind was to build and own twenty-five thousand houses for their ''overspill''. This would mainly be in Dagenham with the border towns of Barking and Ilford, who both had Urban powers to better withstand the impact, than Dagenham's simple Parish Council to take the largest responsibility. Such strain upon the Local Council was ignored by the LCC, who claimed their responsibility stopped at building the houses and roads. It should have been obvious, the village property was old and contained few public buildings from which to direct operations to comply with such an impact. By 1926 a political Labour Party Urban Council was elected by the new residents, demanding normal Social Services for a town structure. Through the years they struggled on to finally obtain, Borough Council status. Up to this time the village had continued to retain something of its original identity.

The many councillors who possessed no sentimental feeling toward the ''old village'' were quite keen to see its soul exterminated, to unite the new town. With all good intentions they accepted a plan to demolish the old and small cottages and rehouse the occupants into new estates they had built. The final

9

blow to exterminate the village came around 1960 when a plan was accepted to compulsorily obtain all private and business premises that formed the remainder of the village, demolish and cram as many new dwellings as possible, certainly with no regard to featuring buildings such as the Old Vicarage or the Parish Church, or even the historic listed "Cross Keys". They have certainly left them alone, and that is just what they look like.

At times we have read and heard of Council's intentions to landscape the whole church area, as with Barking's redevelopment, who no doubt feel justly proud of their very old church area.

How often I have heard folk lament upon the way the old village was redeveloped. I am sure many planners have learned much since. The LCC Aveley Estate, has not unduly disturbed its village. Certainly the LCC huge "Harold Hill Estate" never disturbed Romford or Brentwood. For abnormal rapid housing demands, new towns as Milton Keynes, are preferred, so one can only hope, that the sacrifice paid by Dagenham village has been a lesson to modern planners.

VILLAGE LIFE

Knowing something of my family's long association with Dagenham Village life, for nearly two hundred years, and that my grandfather and subsequently my own father were members of the Parish Council since its formation in 1894, until 1926 when it was superseded by Urban status and represented by a political party; I would like to try and relate some of my own memories of the village, mostly before 1926.

In a village of only a few thousand inhabitants, most families knew something about each other for good or bad; that I am sure acted as a curb to defend one's own reputation.

We were cut off from Barking and Romford, by some four miles of farmland. There were no buses, but a LMS Southend to Fenchurch Street steam train service of possibly six or eight trains each way per day to stop at Dagenham Station. Seldom did a family move out, or a new family take up residence. Many men locally worked on the farms, or at the Sterling Telephone and Radio Factory in Rainham Road. They employed several hundreds during the mid 1920s, although it did appear that many came from Barking and East Ham, for each evening a steady stream could be seen leaving the factory to catch the time-appointed steam train at Dagenham Station. During their boom time with the coming of radio, they built the multistorey steel-framed factory, (that still remains as a social club). Two external lifts were operated, while the building was in full productive use, until 1932 when they transferred their works to Hayes. Also, within the dock area, where the William's Company had created a more lucrative and exciting employment, by developing the docks, for they had also built

11

some small factories, and by 1908, they had helped to persuade the Railway Company to build a station to serve the area, with sidings for their own locomotive system. No one would dare to underestimate their enterprise and the effect they made upon a sleepy village, for they also built two long rows of houses for their employees near the station. The first was known as "Coaly Row" presumably for many that worked on the coal boats, and at right angles a little larger type house, known as "Piano Row" which had a front room large enough to include a piano for those whose job would run to it. They also employed a Mr Freestone to cycle round to their casual employees' homes, to urgently alert them when a coal boat had docked and to report for work immediately. At the end, nearest the station a little general shop was attached that I remember was managed by a Mrs Edwards a proper "oasis in the desert". All has since been demolished.

There were no such places as Labour Exchanges or Job Centres in the 1920s; men would stand outside a factory gate at a specified time to be called in if required or they would be seen standing by the road side in small groups. Two groups of which I remember would be under the thatch roof at the top of Crown Street, another near the church opposite Station Road, (Exeter Road).

They would appear a mixture of men needing a job, talking to older men retired from work. A possible employer would notice and approach them, or a mate would observe them and direct them to a job. A sort of "Labourers for Hire in the Marketplace".

A common sight would be a group of women returning home from a day's work in the fields. They would be conspicuous with their large straw bonnets, which protected their heads from the sun and rain, heavy-duty skirts, laced-up boots and carrying a cane basket on their arms. They sought wages, not for "Mod-Cons", for there were not any, but to honourably repay their tradesmen, who had been good enough to have given them 'credit' during the winter months. Such families as the "Exalls, Bevis, Bush and Ives", readily come to mind for they were able to retain respect for their families, largely through their own efforts.

Like most villages we would have the occasional visit of a

travelling fair or circus. "Col. Print" with the "Bibby's", would settle themselves down at "Crooksies" of which I always understood was common land at the bottom of Dewey Road bordering the railway line. The exciting steam fair organ music, playing "Where do flies go in winter time, Oh' " came upon the village loud and clear, acting like a magnet.

The strong village lads would seek the opportunity to knock off a few coconuts and even smash one to divide amongst the envious kids that stood around, encouraging them, whilst the mums would mount their children upon the gorgeously painted horses on the roundabouts and the swingboats. As for the circus, after parading their animals round the village, they would erect a large marquee on the same site, that boys could brag they were able to climb under the canvas walls, thus save paying at the entrance.

There were also a few occasions when a fair would set up at the rear of the Bull Inn public house; it was known as the Bull Meadow. It was also the scene for quoit matches, by throwing a large iron quoit into a mud pack to compete; a fairly noisy game as one quoit hit the other.

Until 1920 very few motor cars were seen on the road around Dagenham, and for a time we knew the farmers, publicans and doctors who would drive through the village with a single letter on their number plate. Most folk would depend on a pony, trap or a bicycle.

It was quite an event for a family to make a train journey, first to check the time of departure and then all walk together to the station. Invariably to be greeted by Stationmaster Watson, conspicuously dressed in his uniform of dark blue frock coat, a round hat with a gold braided peak. He would take up his place on the platform, remove his gold hunter watch from his vest pocket to make sure that the twelve-fifteen left at twelve-fifteen! The sound of a train pulling out of the station was as reliable a timepiece as the BBC pips are now.

Whilst walking along Church Elm Lane to Ford School in the morning, it was possible to see and hear the ten to nine leaving, and even read its four-figure number painted in large figures on the side of the engine. Such was an assurance that we would arrive at school on time. The station also offered a parcel service, to be received and placed in the guard's van of

Dagenham Railway Station
Note the two milk churns deposited each day by West Ham Rookery Farm

The first village bus service — Bull Inn bus stop
Driver proud of his white coat
Rookery Farm cow sheds are seen almost adjoining

the next passenger train, to be collected from its destined station. For larger cargo, there were gates leading from the station yard, onto the platform, about where the guard's van would stop and there was the goods' yard where the "sidings" would enable to load and unload the trucks. They also engaged a contracting delivery service round the village of which the Gidden Brothers were responsible.

About 1923, the village became very excited at the commencement of the very first village bus service. More so, as it made the Romford journey far more simple. It was introduced by the National Bus Company, with stairs outside to an open top with waterproof aprons to cover the seats if it rained. The route was from the "The Ordnance Arms" at Aveley via Dagenham Bull Inn, then to Romford via Becontree Heath. It was so well received that some folk would travel simply for an exciting ride out.

Most tradesmen continued to use horse and cart to deliver their goods, to outlying farms and cottages. Builders' men would be seen pushing a two-wheeled handcart, with their ladders and materials, also Scouts with the whole troop pulling ropes attached to their handcart containing their camp gear. Box tricycles were in use for Aladdin Dry Cleaners to collect and deliver from the Chequers Corner. Bridges Radio would collect and deliver, recharged accumulators for the early wireless sets. As a village, we had our share of street traders that would make their weekly visits.

One of the Cotgrove family from Leigh would tramp round the village on a Saturday dressed in a blue fisherman's jersey and round peak cap with a large tray of shellfish perched on his head to serve customers at their front door.

A rather nervous fellow would call, "Music, music" as he tried to sell sheet music from a selection he carried on his arm. There was quite a demand then, for one's indoor entertainment was largely confined to playing the piano, or a gramophone.

Another fellow would arrive with a trap loaded with wild rabbits, which were sold as they were, or skinned in the streets invariably for a dog or two standing by in anticipation. Providing a free service if he kept the skin. Then there was always the old scissor grinder and the repairer of cane chairs.

He would sit outside a house with his bag of canes and carry out his repairs, and of course the muffin man with his tray of muffins on his head, ringing a bell to call his customers; a real treat for tea.

Police transport was limited to a bicycle, except for a mobile stretcher mounted on two cycle-type wheels. A constable could be seen pushing it through the streets, mostly to remove a body, that had drifted down the river and washed up on the dock foreshore, to place it in the public mortuary in Church Lane. The fact that it was completely covered over always aroused our morbid curiosity as to whom it might be. A few days later a man, possibly a dock hand, would call upon my father to claim the five shillings that he was authorised to pay on behalf of the Parish Council for anyone who would report the finding of a dead body. Presumably folk were reluctant to get involved. A far less morbid use that would provide us children with a giggle, would be to watch the return of "Old Shimmer" an habitual drunkard practically laying flat out on the stretcher on his way back to the police station to dry out, for his head was not covered and we could recognise him.

Another sad sight would be the "Fever Cab", a single-horse cab complete with nurse and bright red blanket, calling from Rush Green Isolation Hospital to collect a child from a family we knew, that had contracted scarlet fever or diphtheria, fearing they may never return. All such performances were so obvious in the small village. One such family were the Jacksons that lived in Church Street, for in the summer of 1929 they lost two children within one week; James (fourteen years) and Harold (five years). They were nursed at "Rush Green" and sadly returned home to be buried in the village churchyard. With Dagenham's rapidly increasing child population it became a very sad and anxious time for many parents, for at one time it appeared that the town was losing as many children as adults. Fortunately, with the aid of inoculations et cetera, most children's infections were brought under control. By 1940 the Rush Green Isolation Hospital was able to convert to a general nursing hospital.

By 1920, most homes were now connected to the main sewer, but there remained a few remote cottages and farms that were using cesspools of which the Parish Council were responsible for emptying. This was made possible by a horse-drawn iron tank to collect and dispose of in some remote place; I never tried to discover just where. All I remember was the sight and smell of the old "Soil Tank" was not a pleasant experience through the village, and was certainly considered the most menial of tasks.

To complete the village transport, the old hand pump two-wheeled fire engine was kept in a lean-to shed adjoining a row of cottages in Station Road. The Firmans, who kept pigs, chickens and horses in part of the Vicarage Field, were responsible to supply a horse at the shortest notice, being so near and handy. The firemen were all volunteers, and most lived very nearby. I think of such men as Hopkins, Bennett and the Chaplins, for they had an iron plate by their front door which read "Fireman". A very crude affair compared with today's service, but it was a very welcomed effort when needed.

Upon the death of a local inhabitant, a family would avail themselves of the age-old custom, to toll the church bell. For a fee of one shilling and sixpence the sexton would toll the bell during the following day. The code would be able to indicate a man or woman, by three times two for a man, two times three for a woman and the use of the treble bell for a child. The old custom dropped out in the early 1920s as the population began to increase. I am not sure if such a custom still exists in any village today? Apart from peeling the bells for Sunday service and a practice night, one man could chime out simple hymn tunes from a set of ropes encased in the belfry.

Most of our outdoor entertainment centred around the Parish Church. The vicar would hold a Garden Party for a cross section of villagers; also fêtes and sports days, as we only had the Vicarage Field. Men would volunteer to erect sideshows and sports equipment, and appear to enjoy all the effort they put into such communal events. Within the field was the large wooden-built Church Hall that was used for the Church Lads' Brigade; also concerts and bazaars. The only other large hall was the Drill Hall in Rectory Road that could be used, it was owned by the Essex Regiment and had a firing range attached. The vicar, Reverend G. Jones would command great respect as he walked around his parish, eminently dressed in black clerical frock coat, striped trousers, spats and a round hat, and more often trailing his umbrella.

Farmers, apart from paying his tithes, would drop a bag of potatoes and other produce at the vicarage, and it was generally known then that the Samuel Williams' family would make sure he was not short of coal to heat the large vicarage. As children we were made to respect him, for he would frequent our day-school in compliance with its founder (William Ford), who bequested that all children should be offered Church of England Teaching including the Catechism and be able to recite it at an annual examination by the vicar, or the Reverend Pemberton Barnes of Havering, for which we got a half day's holiday to celebrate our interest.

The few policemen that were needed to keep such a small village in order lived with their families and were well accepted as part of village life. Such officers who come to my mind are "Crips, Warne, Stains, Ware, Walker, Lyle, Farrow, Davey and Station Sergeant Cook", who lived at the station. They always appeared to be friendly with us as children, except if they had reason to reprimand us by a flick of their thick woollen gloves, or what was by far more of a threat by saying "I think I will have to have a word with your father about you".

As far back as 1908, the village found the need to set up a trust to purchase one hundred cane chairs that could be hired out for any function that requested them. They were stored in a loft over the porch in Ford's School under the care of the headmaster, Mr Doubleday, and as boys we had to help get them down and return them. My father was the secretary and he was supported by Farmer William Gay and dock executive Harry Bailey as trustees. The service continued up to 1926 when the village became independent of them; a small charge was made to cover repairs and replacement.

As village residents we enjoyed such liberties as to wander into meadows and walk along the foreshore around the dock area, including the Gulf (now covered by the Ford Motor Works Factory). It is hard to imagine what an attractive area it was, producing plenty of fine quality reeds for the local thatchers' work and to supply even the surrounding villages. Within its still waters some very good fishing was possible, even to the extent that city men would enjoy a day at Dagenham's Gulf. They could be seen walking from the dock

Wooden Airship Hangar, built by my father's firm in 1903
for aeronautical experiments around the Gulf area

station with their fishing rods to be observed from the Chequer's Inn by telescope, so that they may count just how many they could expect for lunch.

It also provided a desirable area for the early experiments with aircraft, submarines and airships. A man named "Roberts" appeared in charge, who made contact with my father a village carpenter to repair a plane's wing struts or propeller; odd pieces were kept in our workshop for many years after. They also engaged him to build a very large wooden shed to house an airship. I am sure my father and his partner gained far more from the excitement than any possible profit making.

I understand a recent book was written giving more detail of all that was carried on at the Gulf, during that period.

When in the early 1920s, the London County Council sought government powers and assistance to build some twenty-five thousand houses for their postwar overspill, upon the farmland of Dagenham, the shock to the local Parish Council was unbelievable and beyond their comprehension. The fact that they would have to be responsible for its social and political structure seemed insurmountable. Up to that time all such responsibility was under the control of the Romford Rural District Council, who had already made some small attempt at council house building, with the Marsh Green Estate, which was small enough to fit into the existing service and amenities, and yet even that was not easy to accept.

The big change came in 1926 when they were granted urban powers to contend with the enormous influx of population to provide social services and a town structure. The houses were owned and maintained by the LCC, who clipped the privet hedges with perfect uniformity and collected the rent at various local rent offices. Although the local council benefited by the large rate payment.

Dagenham Council has continued to be made up of strong socially-minded men and women capable of demanding and providing such services as clinics, libraries, parks and swimming pools, to the extent that by 1938 they were able to obtain Borough Council status, to compare quite favourably with its neighbours. Many that worked so hard to achieve such a formidable task, have passed on, but not without leaving their names upon various clinics and old people's homes and roads to bear testimony of their selfless effort for the town. Before the local council were able to supply enough of their own Welfare Service, all sorts of efforts were made by voluntary public-minded residents to supply the needs of its people.

One such that I remember well, was a successful clinic started by the local doctor's wife, Mrs Prosser Evans, who with the help of a few willing ladies met in the old Dagenham Methodist School Room. One half day a week they would invite mothers to bring their babies to be weighed and accept a small supply of virol nutriment dipped out of a large can, into their own cup. Also some helpful advice was offered for the mothers' benefit. All was entirely free. She was also able to arrange a day out for the mothers and their babies to Clacton or Maldon by charabanc.

Charabanc outing to Clacton, 1923
Mrs Prosser Evans is standing at the front

By the First World War, Lloyd George had introduced a stamp card payment from working men that enabled them free medical treatment leaving out their wives and children, who would often deny themselves rather than find payment for doctors' bills; and so the clinic spread to offer them a service, by the means of a voluntary house-collecting scheme of a small amount per month to enable a mother to avail themselves of a district nurse in their home when required. So successful was the scheme that by 1930 the Duchess of York was able to open York House in Frizlands Lane, as a home for district nurses and their training, which was eventually superseded by the coming of the Welfare State. It is now used as a centre for the handicapped. With one of the highest birth rates in the country and well before maternity hospitals were introduced, most babies were born in their own homes. The midwifery service was in great demand. Such folk as Nurse Goddard, Anchor and Rothwell are a few names that come to my mind for they must have had to work very hard in their time.

Long before the days of government "hand-outs" all kinds of means to help each other through difficult times were introduced; such as the Order of Buffaloes, Oddfellows, Ancient Order of Foresters and Railway Men's Union. All were well accepted by men, as some form of security. In the early days they would parade through the streets to promote their cause, with their elaborate banners, marching behind the village band.

Many village folk used the Grays Co-operative Society Store, which was originally formed to look after the working man and his family. A year's dividend shown on the passbook, could well set the children up with new clothes, which was of great value to a mother to find her trading with the society, had so gifted her, as to give a little independence above her husband's wages. Should a working tradesman die, quite often his mates would sell his tools amongst themselves so as to offer his wife a little extra generous support.

Extended payments were rarely available to the working folk. Newly-weds would be eager to snap up the furniture from a home that had to be 'broken up' and the possibility of securing a tenancy needed discreet and swift action for the demand was

1 / 18 **ENGLAND.**

26 Weeks ending 30 June, 1918.

No. in Society _____

Name (Surname) *Throwgego Walter William*

Address in full { *High St* *Dagenham Essex* }

2nd Week, commencing 7 Jan., 1918.

NOTE.—On change of address, the Card should be altered and the Society should be informed within 7 days.

Any Contribution payable at the rate of 6d. must not be paid on this Card. (See Instruction No. 4.)

29 JUN 1918   29 JUN 1918   29 JUN 1918

29 JUN 1918   29 JUN 1918   29 JUN 1918

20th Week commencing 13 May, 1918.

ARREARS FOR WEEKS OF UNEMPLOYMENT MUST NOT BE PAID ON THIS CARD.
(SEE INSTRUCTION No. 8.)

21st Week commencing 20 May 1918	22nd Week commencing 27 May, 1918.	23rd Week, commencing 3 June, 1918.	24th Week, commencing 10 June, 1918.	25th Week, commencing 17 June, 1918	26th Week, commencing 24 June, 1918

The Insured Person should sign in the space below before returning the Card

Signature of Insured Person _____

Address to which future letters { should be sent { _____

National Health Insurance Stamp Card, 1918 — 7d per week
Lloyd George Scheme for the employed only

great, with no possibility to buy or any council house to rent in those days, and many "tied" to their particular employment.

There were a few charities under the control of the vicar and his wardens, that were handed out with discretion. Also young men could avail themselves of a grant towards a Bound apprenticeship, from the "Uphill's Charity". The main assistance was under the control of the Board of Guardians, they were made up of what was known as overseers, elected from the various parish councils within the Romford District. Their main establishment was known as the Romford Union and Infirmary, that had superseded the Parish Workhouse in Workhouse Lane (now Reede Road), many years before my time. Its purpose was dictated by the government to provide for the poor, old and infirmed to be accepted and cared for. They were also to contribute some menial task in return if they were able. Such was in being in most towns in the country. There was attached a casual unit, to provide for tramps, which up to 1930, could be seen waiting in the hedges opposite the infirmary, where they would hide money or any valuables they did not wish to reveal. At six in the evening they would enter for a bath, bed and breakfast, some menial work chopping fire wood or breaking stone, and then out on the road to tramp to the next retreat. There was also what was known as the "RO" (Relieving Officer), that came from the Board of Guardians to interview the poor and needy of the village in the front room of a house in Bull Street, one half-day per week.

As such, the poor were dealt with until things changed and the government took charge of any that were in need. Then the Romford Infirmary became a nursing hospital known as Oldchurch. This was something entirely new, for up to that time sick folk were visited by their doctor and mostly nursed at their home by a relative or friend. If an operation was needed it would have meant a journey to a London hospital and return home for nursing. Most people would, therefore, finally die in their own home, whereupon the village undertaker would be sent to bring a coffin, preferably after dark, to be set up in the front room and remain for a few days, when the family would assemble and be organised by the undertaker to walk to the churchyard, in order of family pairs behind the coffin usually carried by relatives and friends and led by the undertaker, and

Crown Street (looking down)
Left: Arthy's, Bank, Co-op, Soden's, Broadway's, Winch's
Right: White Buildings of Bales Tavern, Family Almshouses, Payne's Butchers

after the burial in the churchyard, to return in the same order. For distance funerals, or if people could afford them, horse-drawn carriages would be hired from a Barking firm.

I feel now if you so wish we could take a walk down through the main village street starting at the top of Crown Street during the early 1920s.

A walk down Dagenham Village street

Walking down Dagenham Village street in the early 1920s, from the High Road, we would find most shops on the south side.

The first would be R. W. Bead's Retail Supply Shop, serviced by his large Hornchurch bakery. Passing a few small cottages, the homes of the Bennetts, Chesney and Cootes. Arthy's carriageway led down to their bakery and stables. Their shop was always in great demand. The family lived in the adjoining house to which was attached a branch of Barclays Bank. The manager would arrive by train on certain days carrying his Gladstone bag to attend the limited business required. Mr and Mrs Tom Palmer were resident caretakers. Then followed the Grays Co-operative Grocery Store known as "The Stores", immediately attached was Ellis' Oilshop, but this soon changed to Crows' Drapery, who for a time took over the Post Office which included the first and only public telephone — "Rainham 1". This was always in use, for there were very few folk with a private telephone, and many small businesses would use it. Soden's most attractive Sweet Shop came next followed by Broadway's Butcher Shop, Tidders' Shoe Repair Shop and Rayment's Greengrocery, subsequently Winches to end the block. A wide carriageway divided a large old black-boarded house, home of the "Jacksons"; they kept horses and pigs, well to the rear of their house. Curly Waite also lived there with his daughter, Maggie, and farmed a small field at the back to grow flowers such as pansies and daisies, which they sold at Stratford Market. Continuing down the hill passed the Playle's house, a short terrace of cottages where "Wag Read" lived, known as "Borritts Cottages". A few brick steps led down to the brook which ran under the road, whereby heavy rainfall would bring it nearer to the top.

Passing over and on the same side, within a large garden, stood a quaint old corrugated iron house; home of the Suffields and Harringtons with a small wooden shed in the front garden to house the village's first "Model T Ford Car". Next was a detached house called Kendrick House, where the Allmans lived. Then we came to a really old-fashioned little cottage with an iron framed front door, where Mrs Allerton lived. She offered a dressmaking service for the ladies of the village who would take their own material for her to work with. Then a few more very old cottages; Ivy Cottage with its unusual text written on the side of the house, it was one that I have never forgotten, it read, "Tomorrow, Today, will be our Yesterday". I never knew what the origin was, but this was all demolished in 1930 and a street market was planned by Shifes Market Ltd.; however, this never materialised. Then came the

Crown Street (looking up from the brook)

Parish Church with its walled churchyard built on the edge of the road, with a side gate, but no pavement. As it met with Church Street it widened out for the church main entrance. Anthony Goddard's loaded coal cart could be seen outside his old black-boarded house.

To cross over and return down the north side, one could step down into Kirks Hardware Shop, that many years previously, my great-grandfather had bought and carried on a harness maker's business. Adjoining was known as the "Keys Alley" which led down to the Vine Cottages, homes of the Hawkins and Sayers. It was always closed to traffic once a year, by two beer barrels and a plank, to claim to Cross Key rites during which time the old public house that had obtained historic interest was very well maintained by the highly respected Poston family. Their garden-boarded fence extended down to the high wall which enclosed the seventeenth century vicarage.

Cottage and Shop next to Cross Keys
See Sale Notice

Lot 1.

A FREEHOLD PROPERTY,

COMPRISING

A 'CAPITAL SHOP,

With Ware-room at back, Sitting Room, Kitchen and Four Rooms over, Stable, Cart Shed, and Large Garden,

Let to Mr. East, at per Annum, £16. 0s.,

ALSO

A DWELLING ADJOINING,

Containing Two Rooms and Kitchen on the *Ground Floor*. And Two Rooms on the *First Floor*. Shed at the Side, lately used as a Forge, and Garden with Shed.

Let to Mr. Twyford, at per Annum, £12.

SITUATED

In the Best Part of the Village of Dagenham, Opposite the Church, about Two Miles from Rainham Railway Station,

[handwritten text, largely illegible]

Sale Notice, 1861
Premises bought by my great-grandfather, Edward John West
Note: Near Rainham Station before Dagenham had a station

Continuing down the hill, a few more small cottages where Sherby Waites also grew flower roots and watercress within the brook, to join Allen's Paper Shop, which for a time also served as a post office. Well before my time it had been converted from a public house "The Good Intent". After passing over the brook again another small row of cottages, with a tree that hung over the road, lived a Miss Tilly Stafford. Her father had been a village Master Bricklayer of some repute, and her front room was let to Doctor Gibbons from Barking as his local surgery. His old Harley-Davidson motor bike parked outside was evidence of his ability to attend to his patients. At the far end of the block another quaint little bay window shop, to step down into, known as Johnnie Brown's, containing every hardware article possible — an "Oilshop". Leaving that most

Crown Street (looking up from the Almshouses)
Manor Farm is at the top of the street

intriguing little store. Payne would exhibit most of their meat outside the sawdust-covered shop floor. Almost adjoining, was a row of almshouses which stood at right angles with the road. They had been gifted by the Coymns family, successful local tanners, many years previously. Then passing Stacey's Fish Shop where one was offered fried pieces of fish for 2d, 3d, 4d, and leave with a penny worth of chips. Then to look in at Sproits Barbers' Shop with their striped pole outside, offering a shave for twopence, haircut sixpence. We then come to a pair of gates leading to Bales Horse Cartage Yard and Stables. The two or three cottages were originally part of the old public house, the Rose and Crown, converted home of the Bales family; then Granny Wellington's old-fashioned bay window extending well onto the pavement, which apart from another small cottage, home of the Tibbles family, brought us to Stebbings Butcher Shop, that had a thatched roofed slaughter house attached which extended round the corner to the High Road. That would complete a return trip down Crown Street and back, during the early 1920s.

VILLAGE SCHOOLING

Although my father had told me of his experience at attending "The Little Infants' School" in Church Lane, for which his father paid twopence per week, when I started in 1913 The New Infants' School as we knew it, had been built by The School Board, some thirty years previous, and taken over by The Essex County Council. With Ford's Endowed School very well established, schooling became a simple matter of attending the two schools well equipped, and both in Church Elm Lane.

The roads were comparatively quiet, and all we children, were known well in the village and had no fears to walk on our own to and from school; even home to dinner. We enjoyed the journey to play with marbles, whip and top or bowl our hoops; little traffic. The Infants' School Governess was a Miss Huntly. I cannot recall much of the routine, except that we were taught plain knitting, as it was during the First World War. I believe I was eight years old when, with all my mates we were taken along the road and handed over to Mr Harry Verney, Ford's School Headmaster. From a large Assembly Hall, the classrooms led off with half-glass doors. Each room was heated by large open coal fires with iron guards around them. It would be the bigger boys' job to take the scuttle outside to the coal shed, break large lumps, to return it to the fireplace.

The teacher would use the blackboard and easel while we sat in pairs, at our desks which formed a locker. Each had an inkwell to dip our pens in; also to use blotting paper, for there were no such pens as Biros.

31

Ford Endowed School, Church Elm Lane
Now Demolished

We were taught to read music, by hanging a modulator sheet over the blackboard, by singing the scale Do, Ra, Me, etc. All our exercise books had the Essex County logo printed on them; three daggers. The playground had little in it, apart from two walnut trees. A large thermometer hung on the wall advertising ''Stephen's Ink''. There was a brass water drinking tap with an iron mug chained to it, and an open-sided play shed if it rained, with outside lavatories. The boys' and girls' playgrounds were separated. In the corner of the playground there was a section of garden plots, for the older boys to train on. One or two attempts were made to enforce a uniform, but without any assistance, most were too poor to afford it. All boys wore short trousers until they left school at fourteen years, and would be jeered at if they appeared in long trousers, ''yer longans''. In my early school days, most boys wore large ''Eton collars''. Examinations were carried out fairly simply, and an annual report prepared and given out unsealed

Dagenham Ford's Endowed School

Report (Xmas Term 1920)

Name _ J. West _____   Standard _ 4

Subject	Maximum Marks	Marks obtained	Progress, conduct etc
Arithmetic	20	0	V. weak in Arith: &
Reading	20	8	Spelling.
Handwriting &c	20	11	
English Lit	20		Done well in Oral
Composition	20	9	subjects. —
Geography	20	20	
History	20	20	
Drawing	20	6	Conduct
Needlework	20		V. Fair
Brushwork	20	12	
Recitation	20	7	
Spelling	20	14	
Totals	200	104	

Number examined __ 59   Position in class __ 42c

Class Teacher _ Mr. _ Chase

Elementary School Report, 1920 — Note large class (59)
A poor show — left plenty to improve upon!
It's easy to laugh now

c

to show your parents if you were not too ashamed of it. Several of our teachers were from local families and just stayed on, without going to college. We were seldom given homework. There were occasions when the headmaster would cane a seriously offending boy in front of the assembled school. Once a week the senior boys would attend a woodwork class in a special building within the infants' school, which was also used by the girls for cookery lessons.

From 1914—1925, my elementary education was very simple indeed, although no doubt it had improved a little from the previous generation. There were two or three scholarships handed out each year, for the brainy kids to attend ''The Royal Liberty'' or ''The County High School for Girls''; both at Romford. Marsh Green School was also in Dagenham, but mainly served the New Road and Dock area.

As the village, we had very little to do with the school. Also there were evening classes outside the district for those keen to learn.

When one visits the modern Comprehensive Schools today, with their vast range of subjects and equipment to fill the brain with, I can't help but feel our brains got let off very lightly in comparison; yet in spite of a simple elementary schooling, many I know of, my own limited schooling, have risen to very responsible positions, which seems to prove it is largely up to the individual, for there are always opportunities after leaving school to go on learning.

ROADS

Long before I can remember, apparently the roads were maintained by the bordering farmers, as were the hedges and the ditches, to drain off the water from the road. Gravel was dug from a road-side pit. One such pit was eventually filled in to erect the Methodist Church Sunday School building in 1934.

My earliest recollection was when the Romford Rural District Council were responsible for Dagenham's road surfacing. A steamroller with heavy chisels attached to churn up the road and lay granite chippings to be rolled level. Then some years later came the tar spraying, covered with a fine shingle, that when freshly laid, caused small stones to fly up, from passing vehicles.

Of the few jobs allotted to the Parish Council, was the cleaning of the roads, also lighting, collecting of the household rubbish, and to empty the few remaining cesspools from the remote parts of the village. For the roads, the Council employed a "Road Sweeper", his name was Mr Hunt, as I remember, who would walk around the village with a wooden "Navy Barrow" broom and shovel. As he spent most of his time on the road, folk would be able to contact him, to ask if he had seen a CERTAIN person. I well remember my father riding his cycle round the roads, and being quite relieved to have found my four-year-old brother, being cared for by the road sweeper.

As for lighting the roads, which was little better than nothing, for there were only a few lamps at strategic points, to the extent that inhabitants would heckle parish councillors at

election meetings, accusing them of arranging lampposts
outside their own residences. It all sounds so petty now, but
they were serious. I do not remember oil lamps for street
lighting, but gas mantles had to be lit, and put out each day.
The Parish Council employed a man both willing and able to
carry out the duty reliably. The two young fellows that I
remember were "Amos" and "Godfrey". They would ride
around on their bikes with a long brass pole, which included a
burning flame to push the tap on and light the lamp and repeat
the journey later to put them out. After a time the bypass was
introduced, which simplified the job, to just push on and push
off. Carts would carry oil or candles; cars used oil lamps until
carbide acetylene came in for a short time — a form of portable
gas lamp. It would not be an unusual sight to see folk carrying
a lantern along the road, for in those days when it was dark,
there was no London glow, you could see the stars and
welcome the light from the moon.

Flint's Farmyard, for rubbish collection
On the corner of Frizlands Lane and Bull Lane
Now Demolished

As for the Council's responsibility to collect the household rubbish, they employed a contractor, the "Flint" family. They had horse and carts to collect and deal with it at their yard at the top of Frizlands Lane. When one realises in those days there was very little food packaging and every house had an open fire, and thought nothing of lighting a "Bonfire". Also most families kept chickens or pigs to eat up any vegetable peelings. A small village never found rubbish disposal a major problem, for the "Rag Man" would *pay for* "The Rubbish" he collected.

Back to roads. On going to school in the 1920s, we would make good use of the gutters, for they formed a basis for such games as "Marbles" or "Whip and Top". We would also make full use of the roads to bowl our metal hoop with a skimmer. We were more than willing to run an errand. If we heard a car coming we would try and guess who it was, for there were only a few, and they were owned by doctors, farmers or publicans.

A familiar sight on the road, would be a farm wagon returning home in the afternoon from a London market, having delivered a full load of vegetables the night before. The driver would be laid out across the seat, asleep, leaving the horse to make its all too familiar way home to the farmyard. Another sight would be a fast horse, with its driver seated upon little more than a pair of wheels, out exercising from Parsloes Trotting Park.

The main roads were High Road (now Rainham Road South), the section of road from Becontree Heath to Rainham, it included the railway station, police station and the village's only resident doctor (Prosser Evans). At the corner of Manor Road, it branched down into the village for shopping. It was known as Crown Street, with shops on either side, down the hill, over the bridge, that one could go down a few steps to draw a can of water when visiting the churchyard; up the hill past the Parish Church leaving the seventeenth century vicarage on the opposite side to reach Church Street, with another parade of shops, and the Smithy on the south side; through Church Elm Lane to pass both Infants' and Ford's School to reach the Church Elm Public House, which formed a 'T' junction. A road from the dock area, passed through Broad

Street over the railway bridge along Halbutt Street toward Becontree Heath. At a junction a road led down Oxlow Lane to meet the High Road. It was known as Wantz Corner, with a house on the edge of the road with a white stone double step, by the road side. Some said it was to protect the house from carts turning; others suggested it was there to assist one to remount their horse if they had difficulty. Beyond where the High Road joined Crown Street, was known as Bull Street, mainly consisting of small cottages with the Methodist Church and opposite, my home "The White House", a very old seventeenth century farmhouse. On past the Bull Inn, leaving the Old Rookery farmhouse and cow shed on the same side. To reach another very old house "Stoneford Cottage" which is listed of historic value, the home of the "White" family for many years. Following on just before one reached the Rom River (the village boundary), an ambitious venture had been started around 1875 to build a canal from the Thames to Romford and at great expense a brick bridge was built upon the road. By the outbreak of the First World War, the whole work was suspended. When, by 1920 the village tried to get back to normal, motor transport had become destined for road haulage; ex-army Pierce Arrow lorries were soon seen through the village carting gravel, to build the Barking Power Station. Road transport had come to stay, and so the canal venture had ceased to be an economic project. The bridge and original cutting remained for many years, with no water. Children would enjoy playing under it, until between 1950—1960 when it was demolished due to extensive road widening. A trace of the cutting is still visible on the south side of the road.

The only real use of the bridge we enjoyed, was to take our sledge down in the winter for some fun, well before motor traffic took over, and when it did, we found even more fun to drive our bull-nosed Morris Tourer at speed, for with little or no shock absorbers, to bounce the occupants up and down for a laugh. It was a humpbacked bridge that never served any real purpose.

FOOTPATHS

There were several footpaths from the village across fields that were continuously used. For most folk had to walk during the day, or even at night, especially if the moon shone. If you passed anybody, you would mostly recognise them and speak to them having no fears, as we would today.

From a stile in the centre of the village, near to where Grays Court is now, started a public footpath to Dagenham Dock. After the first field, then a muddy path known as Marley Causeway, onto another path we now know as Marsh Green Road. It was well used by folk working in the dock area, and in return, for those who needed to visit the village. To miss a train timing at Dagenham Station would often present a quick short cut, to catch a train at the Dock Station, saving possibly an hour in reaching Barking, or similar on return, if timings were better.

Another well-used path, was from the High Road (Rainham Road) across part of Manor Farm, beyond what is now known as the top of Western Avenue, then to cross the main line through crossing gates, more fields to reach what we knew as "Anthony Vincents" of now the Elm Park area. A small part of this public path still exists, between Aldborough Road and Mayswood Gardens. The very well-used path to Romford started over a stile from Stockdales Farm Road, to reach Eastbrook End, then to join the Main Road, that made as direct to reach Romford.

One other that I well remember to reach Becontree Heath, would commence from the centre of the village by walking

Station Road (Exeter Road) through the railway crossing gate, crossing over Workhouse Lane (Reede Road) along a path which led down to Oxlow Lane, that we now know as Hunters Hall Road, and then a direct path through Frizlands Leafy Lane, brought one onto the heath.

While walking at night, it was quite a common sight to see a glow-worm 'illuminated' writhing along the dirt path. Yet there never seemed anything with which to pick it up. Farmers seldom would show any consideration when ploughing their fields, which would annoy folk to retrace the path and in due course flattened the soil, and resurfaced the pathway. The Parish Council would erect direction posts, to maintain the public rights of use. One could even lift a cycle over a stile and ride on, quite accepted. Folk would not be too concerned to meet the village undertakers carrying a coffin to a remote dwelling, which was mostly after dark, for it would have been recognised as where it was destined, in most instances.

FARMS

Manor Farm
The Manor Farmhouse stood at the top of the village (now a parade of shops). The farm was mainly arable to grow cabbages, beans and peas. Whole village families would be invited to spend a day "Pea Picking". Part of the farm,

Manor Farmhouse
At the top of Crown Street and on the corner of Manor Road and Rainham Road
Demolished 1955

41

bordering the road near the "BULL INN" was set aside for allotments that the Parish Council were obliged to provide for its inhabitants. From the farmyard with its barns and cart sheds, a centre path made its way down to the meadows that bordered the Rom River; there was easy access to the fields on either side.

From 1914 the farm was owned and worked by Mr Walter Jones. Around 1924 he sold a few acres to Messrs Balch to excavate sand and gravel. All has since been refilled and used as playing fields. Balch also built on an unexcavated part to form part of "Beamway". The Joneses continued to farm and kept a herd of cows for milk, that was always available at the farmhouse door. By 1925 the population had greatly increased and they began to experience interference about the farm. To stay on would become uneconomical, and so with his four sons, Mr Jones bought a farm at Navestock, and sold Manor Farm to Messrs Alan and Ansel, Speculators and Developers, who planned it into roads and small building plots, with the help of Horshams, a local estate agent, offered them at reasonable prices. Within one year plot holders were asked to pay a few extra pounds to redeem the local vicar's tythe. Some folk who had lost their allotments over the sale, bought a plot to work on. Also many from East Ham or Barking bought plots of 40 × 150 for sixty pounds. They used it for a weekend retreat, and to garden; then in due time were able to build their own permanent home, and so it became known as the Manor Farm Estate.

Although most services were laid, the roads remained grass tracks for many years. It was not until 1960, that the Borough took over and charged for the road surfacing. The several plots, where no owners could be traced, were sold by public auction, to square the road charges accounts. It is now a well-developed estate, with a variety of bungalows and houses, all owner-occupied, except for a few blocks of Council houses in the north-east corner.

Stockdale Farm

The Stockdale Farm bordered the railway line at Dagenham East, nearly back to the Hornchurch boundary. From my earliest recollection, it was farmed by the "Wilkin" family, mainly for fruit growing, currants and stawberries, etc. It was all so open to the High Road (Rainham Road) which tempted us boys to climb in and sit among the bushes without being seen, to help ourselves. As early as 1920, it was rumoured that a chemical factory would one day be built there. Soon after that the "Wilkins" moved to Tiptree to establish their well-known jam factory. But it was let again, tenanted by the Cook family, a retired local police station sergeant, who with his son Bob, set up quite a successful milk round, which continued until 1933.

May and Bakers it was revealed owned "Stockdales" since 1912 and decided to build their factory. With easy access to the railway station, they moved down from Battersea, bringing many of their staff with them. Many settled in the new houses, being built all around them. Edward Glenys had built Gay Gardens, Laws Cherry built Western Avenue houses to sell at £495 each. The factory began to operate and tried hard not to upset their neighbours with their chemical smells, and appeared on very good relations with their employees. Throughout their very successful years of trading, they have continued to build and expand on the site. Only during the last few years have they announced that they are now controlled by a French firm, Rhone-Poulenc.

Rookery Farm

The Rookery Farmhouse stood very near to the Bull Inn, possibly in the middle of the Bull Roundabout. The farm was owned by the West Ham Corporation, and was managed by their bailiff, Mr Tom Maddocks, with his family, to include two sons and three daughters, all of whom were very popular in the village. Within the farm, West Ham had their own isolation hospital, for during the early part of the century, smallpox and tuberculosis, were very rife. It appears the purpose of the farm, was to supply their hospitals with dairy produce, especially milk, although they did grow some corn, which was thrashed annually at the farm. Contractor engineers would arrive with a steam traction engine with a large belt drive. It was fascinating to watch it separate the kernels from the cavings and straw. Which were all by-products for the farmyard.

It was a regular job for Mr Maddocks to drive his horse and

trap down to the railway station each evening with two large churns of fresh milk, to place on the platform, to be picked up by the 5.15 and delivered to Plaistow Station, for their West Ham hospital to collect. We boys, would be permitted to jump up onto the back for a ride. Approximately once each year, members of the West Ham Corporation would visit the farm, comfortably seated in their maroon ceremonial saloon horse-drawn coach and pair, bearing their coat of arms on the side. After surveying the farm and stock they would partake of lunch in the farmhouse, prepared by Mrs Maddocks, part of councillors' perks I suppose.

Rookery Farm, 1921
Annual visit of inspection by West Ham Councillors with their ceremonial coach
Mr Maddocks (in bowler hat) with his two young sons, Charley and Bob
Demolished c. *1950*

The tragic death of Mr Maddocks from a road accident in 1932, severely shook the Corporation, who after a time, appointed his eldest son, Charlie, to carry on in charge of the farm; all appeared quite successful for many years. Soon after the war, the farm had to contend with many intruders and vandals, which prompted the fact that as a farm it had had its day, all of which coincided with West Ham's concern for their overspill of population. By 1948 they submitted plans to Dagenham Council to build an estate of "Prefab" houses of a semi-permanent nature, as opposed to our own local Council's effort, building prefabs with approx ten years' duration. The whole estate proved very successful, for after forty years with a little updating, they appear as good as any.

The Corporation then appeared to have transferred the hospital to the Regional Health Authority. For a time it was used for chronic and geriatric patients, and although it was not necessary for local folk, interest was such that a "Friends of the Hospital" was set up and an Annual Fête to raise funds for extra comforts for the patients. All that remains today is a large derelict site of undeveloped waste ground, owned by Municipal Authority, possibly within the 'Green Belt' area in the extreme south-east border with Havering's land.

Eastbrook Farm
Eastbrook Farm was owned and farmed by the Gay family; Mr William Gay, entered very much into village life, as a Parish Councillor and represented Dagenham as a member of the Romford Board of Guardians.

The farm was mainly arable, growing cabbages, peas and potatoes, later introducing lettuce, helped by water, drawn from nearby pits; all produce for the London markets. As boys, we were invited to spend some of our summer holidays picking up potatoes at piecework rates of 2d per box. In the corner of a field near the Bell House was a road-side pond that horses could be pulled in for a drink. By its side a sunken barrel of ever-running clean spring water, that one could put their cupped hands for a refreshing drink. It continued for many years, then during the 1930s the South Essex Water Works, decided to sink a pipe through the chalk from their Beam Pumping Station. Since, has all been filled, to leave no trace.

Also by the road side near the farm was a quaint little mud house, where "Granny Lazell" lived, it was called "Clay Pug". As time passed more and more of the farm's good land gave way to ballast excavation and the farm became uneconomical to continue. The farmhouse was converted into "The Farmhouse Tavern". It was then, the Gays left Dagenham to farm elsewhere.

Apart from certain pits that have been reserved for fishing, and the establishment of a gypsy encampment, most pits are re-filled, as the whole area falls within the Green Belt, which fails to attract any development interest. Our local Council were able to purchase most of the land for playing fields and open spaces.

Frizlands

The impressive old Frizlands Farmhouse stood facing Frizlands Lane, surrounded by a few labourers' cottages. For very many years it was owned and farmed by Mr Colsum Parish. Fortunately for him it escaped the LCC Compulsory Purchase Order. Yet to continue farming, bordered by so much housing development, became impossible, but greatly increased the value of what was virtually farmland. Several acres were purchased by the Borough Council to build the "Heath Park Estate" of Council houses for letting. A most ingenious plan was devised, to heat the houses from the surplus heat supplied by the huge dust destructors nearby. As the underground pipes continued to leak, the residents formed themselves into an association, to force the Council to amend the whole unsuccessful project, that failed.

Another large part of the farm was sold for a private house development, by Messrs Waites, and was subsequently known as "The Waites Estate". The farmhouse was demolished about 1930 and all the farm covered with houses.

Pound Farm

Pound Farm with its house "Merrilans" was owned by the Samuel Williams Co., as part of their Dagenham Dock Estate. For many years it was tenanted and farmed by Mr Charles Gunnery, who lived there with his family. His land was bordered by the west side of Broad Street, and the south side of

Church Elm Lane, opposite Ford's School, of which Mr Gunnery was a School Governor. During the First World War, he was able to negotiate with Mr Harry Verney, our headmaster, for a class of us boys to "Top" his fill of beans opposite the school due to adult labour shortage. I do recall the fun we got from skipping lessons, which was ample compensation for our efforts. We never knew if our master benefitted or not.

Most of the fields fell within the LCC Compulsory Purchase Order, of which one side of Broad Street, Heathway and Ford Road now include dense housing. The Gunnery family moved into the Old Manor Farmhouse for a time and entered into the village life, forming a local cricket team, near the station. After a time they purchased a farm at Stapleford Abbots, to continue their family occupation.

Home Farm

Home Farm was comparatively small, from what I can recall. It was bordered on the north side by railway lines at Dagenham East and along a few hundred yards of the Rainham Road, where a Mr Chandler carried on a chaff cutting business for local supply, in some sheds opposite Dewey Road. The time when the value of the land greatly increased and gave way to the development of Western Avenue, Mayeswood Gardens by Messrs Laws Cherry who built houses for sale and subsequently "Beadle" built a parade of shops on the Rainham Road.

A large part between Western Avenue and the railway was excavated by "Boyers" — now mainly refilled. During the last war a gun site was built there. For many years now, it has presented a derelict site, for although several attempts have been made to obtain planning permission it has been continually refused, due to the disturbing effect traffic would have upon the bridge and the residents of Western Avenue.

Leys Farm

Leys Farm was bordered by the New Road on the south side and by the Rookery Farm on its east side. It was owned and farmed by Walter Borritt, who could be considered a "Gentleman" farmer, one would have imagined financially independent, for his traps and his own dress could appear immaculate while seen driving through the village. His mostly arable farming produced for the London markets. By 1930, having escaped the LCC Compulsory Purchase Order, he was able to sell several acres to Costains to build their Rylands Estate, mainly for the Ford employees. Houses were offered as low as £400, with easy payments as simple as renting — £25 down, then 18/- per week. It all appeared a very successful venture to meet the demand. Folk would buy to obtain complete control, able to sub-let to the many lodgers eager to avail themselves a residence whilst working at Fords. As for the remainder of the land, the Borough Council purchased most of the rest to lay out the Leys Sports Ground and Swimming Pool, which also includes ground for Ballards Road, main access to Fords Motor Co. The fact the remainder fronted the estate on the east side of Broad Street, greatly increased its value to offer individual shop plots. A trading covered market, a working man's club and a considerable plot purchased by the Grays Co-operative for milk dairy yard and departmental store.

BECONTREE HEATH

Becontree Heath was an extension of Dagenham village with comparatively fewer inhabitants; some lived in caravans within the yards of dealers. They would have addresses as Dennis's Yard or Reader's Yard. The Heath was surrounded by groups of mostly terraced houses, for the more established families as the "Bixbys" or "Readers" many that were dealers. The "Readers" with ample horse and carts would go out as far as Aveley and buy up surplus straw cheap to return to their spacious yards on the Heath and prepare it for sale, to the many London stables.

Men such as Dave Bixby, would journey out as far as the Ockendons, sample a local farmer's field of potatoes ready to harvest, strike a cash deal, being in the fortunate position to transport his local gang of experienced women field workers, all keen to harvest his deal at piecework rates. I suppose all three parties were very satisfied?

With no parish church, no railway station, it seems the Heath was well blessed with three public houses; all so near. "The Three Travellers", "The Ship and Anchor" and "The Merry Fiddlers", and yet with so small houses and large families. I am sure they supplied a need for folk to meet and strike their deals. The families appeared to be quite contented to intermarry, even to the extent that one had to be careful when talking, to realise so much relationship.

The village folk had little doubt that the Heath contained some doubtful characters. They had their own policeman, "Rawson", I seem to remember, who had learned the art of

Becontree Heath (looking west from the Civic Centre)
Left: The Three Travellers; Centre: Ship and Anchor;
Shops: Copsey Harness Maker, Hart's Newsagent, Brewster's Post Office,
Albon's Wheelwright Yard; Methodist Church layed back with Aldridge's Grocery

"Running with foxes and hunting with the hounds", to remain in the job and able to maintain a reasonable state of order.

Although no parish church, the existence of a well-established Methodist Chapel in the centre, cannot be over estimated in its effort to attract some of the more respected families. The Albons, Brewsters and Thorogoods; wheelwright, post office and insurance agent, respectively, who so devoutly upheld the good christian principals which was finally responsible to bring "The Heath" into a highly-respected community, when the great change came for it to be swallowed up, as the village, into a modern town. The largest building (now demolished) was the Day School, it was also used for meetings, which included the first Dagenham Parish Council meetings, consisting of farmers and businessmen, etc.

Until the latter part of 1920, it was a usual sight to see the residents stake their horses and goats out on the grass Heath of which accepted the name of "Nanny Goat Common", later to become a bus stop, that conductors delighted in shouting out, while on route to Romford.

Just how the Council obtained the right to take charge of what was virtually common land, I never knew. I do not recall any organised resistance, for I suppose at the time it appeared the only course to take. To assume an ownership so vital, finding itself set within a fast-developing town, requiring a civic centre, a modern fire station and many other uses they have made of what was the Heath, that is still publicly held, even if the common rites have gone. Flint's old farmyard was on the corner of Bull Lane and Frizlands Lane, for they were contractors to the Parish Council to collect the small amounts of rubbish from the village. Many years ago, the site was developed as a vast dust distructor unit.

TRADESMEN

Burk — Blacksmith

The village blacksmith's workplace was very open and exposed to the general public. It all formed a great attraction to the New Estate folk during the mid 1920s. It was in the centre of the village, opposite Glebe Road. The horses were led into an open stable for Charlie Burk to work on in full view of all those passing. In his shirt sleeves and leather apron, he would pick up the horse's hoof and hold it between his knees. With his tool box at hand he would use his claw hammer to extract the long special nails, throwing the worn shoe aside, then clean and prepare the hoof to receive the new shoe. From his stock he would select the nearest fit, then enter the enclosed part of his workshop to heat it, red hot, in the forge. This resembled a heap of coal dust, to be quickly fanned into a fire when pumped by the large bellows. We boys were often chased out for making the sparks fly, by pumping too furiously. Charlie would take out the red-hot shoe with a long pair of tongs, place it on the anvil and fashion it into shape, his son Ted would strike heavy blows upon a chisel to make the required holes for the nails. It was then fitted to the horse's hoof, of which much smoke and smell was obvious, yet the horse did not appear to worry. Nailed on with the special nails, rasped off clean then painted over with hoof oil, the job was completed.

Apart from shoes there were many other articles produced. Farmers would require a supply of hoes, fashioned as only "Burks" knew how. Builders would require special iron rods and stays. Mr Burk lived with his wife, son Ted and daughter

52

Winnie, in the house attached. By the mid 1930s his trade
became obsolete and he willingly retired. The Smithy's
workshop was demolished, and a row of modern private houses
now cover the ground fronting Church Street.

Flint — Milkman
The Flint family were of very old Dagenham farming stock,
and had kept a dairy farm in Halbutt Street for many years.
Most of which was acquired by the LCC in the early 1920s and
built on to form part of Heathway. They were able to carry on
as tenants, by daily receiving milk from their Shenfield farm by
fast pony cart. Mr Flint himself could be seen daily, in his milk
float standing behind a large churn from which he would fill a
special pail, that included a one pint and half pint ladel to serve
his loyal village customers, at their front doors. By pouring the
required amount into their jugs, all such deliveries were quite
well accepted. As the larger dairy companies improved their

Flint's Milk Cart
A familiar sight about the village until 1950

services and competition, Flints failed to keep pace and failed to satisfy the local authorities and consequently were continually harassed by the Courts. They continued on with the village round. By the mid 1950s they delivered bottles of milk in conjunction with a large dairy, by their own motor van, refusing to be taken over. His sons worked hard and loyal, but never proved equal to modern competition in business, for I am sure they would have been far more able to produce than sell. In spite, they carried on until the mid 1970s, when the Council regained possession and the house was demolished, and the site re-developed.

Dan Bourn — Hairdresser

In the 1920s Dan Bourn lived with his family over his hairdressing shop, on the parade near the church. He had a "Clubbed" foot, not too attractive to us children, but he was generally accepted as a good barber, so we were often made to attend against our will.

The Parade
Palmer's Drapery Store, Dan Bourn Hairdresser, Allen's Sweet Shop,
Miller's Grocery, Warner's Chemist, Acreman's Greengrocery

His shop consisted of two heavy old barbers' chairs, complete with headrests, covered in rexine, with a board standing by to put across the arms for the very young customers. Two large mirrors hung in front of the washbasins, with a shelf to hold his clippers, combs, brushes, and a bottle of scented water that he would spray on to finish the job. Quite conspicuously hung a very polite notice, which read "IF THE RAZOR PULLS — SO TO SPEAK". As shaving formed a large part of his custom, personal brushes and shaving pots were always at hand for "the Regulars".

He had a son who would race home from school, put on his white apron, and take up his job as "Lather Boy", this entailed preparing the waiting customer in the spare chair, for his father to operate on. During 1920—30, men seemed to enjoy a shave at the barber's by open razor, as most found it very difficult to obtain so keen an edge by their own efforts. The introduction of safety razors, as we know them, made a slow progress, to become as universally adopted as today; certainly electric razors were not on the market, but what I am sure made the visit far more acceptable, was, it gave the opportunity to catch up with much unprintable scandal and to review the political situation, providing your barber had the sense to agree with you!

To require a haircut on its own, would be termed as "Robbing the Barber of a shave", for which during that time would be 2d for a shave, 6d for a haircut. It was later that he had to meet competition from the "Sproits", for by offering us kids a bag of sweets, the objectional operation was made much more acceptable.

Soden — Sweet Shop

Soden's Sweet Shop was half-way down the hill in Crown Street, and it was always an attraction to the children. Mr Howard the local sign writer had artistically written his name boldly over the shop, G. SODEN Confectioner & Tobacconist. Mr Soden himself gave the impression of an ex-military man, with a well-trimmed white moustache, and of a spotlessly clean appearance. He would deal with children's requests as if they were of tremendous importance. It was a comparatively small shop; four or five customers would fill the space provided. His

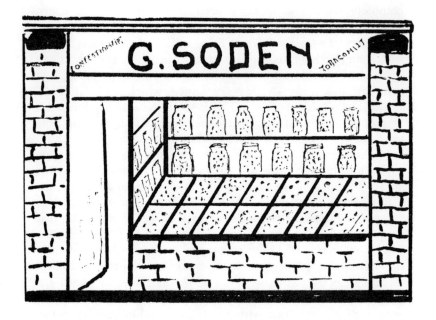

Soden's Sweet Shop
Sketch showing display

shop window would display his selection of sweets; they were laid out in small trays, possibly twenty sections of approx six inches square. There would be "Hazel Nut Creams", "Acid Drops", "Liquorice Comforts", "Tiger Nuts", "Locus Beans", "Bull's-Eyes", "Cough Drops", "Jelly Babies", and "Dolly Mixtures", also a selection of chocolates — all clearly named, and most priced at 4oz — 4d. Upon a shelf at the side, would be paper packets of sherbet and lemonade powder, with a black liquorice straw, also imitation black liquorice smoking pipes and shredded brown coconut as tobacco. He also kept a supply of whips and tops and coloured glass marbles, to bring when such came into season.

The door was mostly open, but a door bell would promptly alert to a customer's presence. The back part of his shop window was shelved to hold the rows of large glass jars of loose sweets, the same as the samples to be taken down when selected, shook into small polished brass scales which he kept on the counter, then placed within a white sweet bag, snatched from a string by his side; then he'd return the jar to its former position. What always appeared far more fascinating was to watch the performance when asking for a half pound slab of Cleves Toffee, for this gave him the opportunity to act with great professionalism, to carefully unwrap the slab, then with his left hand, place it between a special plated cutter, then with a sharp jerk with his right hand, he would neatly divide it into equal pieces to be weighed and placed into a bag, then handed over with great satisfaction at being able to offer such a service.

The tobacco side of his business was separated by a counter flap that he used as an access to his living quarters. Bottles of 'R' Whites mineral water were also available on this side. A quite usual sight would be to see loose tobacco being weighed out from steel jars for pipe smokers. "Woodbine" cheapest cigarettes were sold in open paper packets of five.

"Old Soden" was the children's village hero, for he could always find something for 1d or 2d, which was the accepted child's tip. He had a stepson "Bill Hewitt", who seldom appeared in the shop, for Soden himself was rather exclusive and always served his customers with great respect.

Stebbings — Butchers

At the top of Crown Street, there was a butcher's shop, with a thatched roof slaughterhouse attached. It was owned by the "Stebbing" family, and with Johnny Key in charge of the slaughtering. Around 1925 he could be seen riding his bike with a stick in one hand, to drive home a bullock his governor had bought in Romford Market. Once a week they would receive a couple of fattened pigs, brought up in a cart from Rookery Farm.

My earliest memory would be to see the fresh-dressed animals hung up outside the shop, for passers-by to inspect the quality. The "Stebbings" were also responsible to supply Paynes Butchers at the bottom of the street, who especially at Christmas time, would set out their shop front including the gateway, by laying down straw and exhibiting all his stock of

Crown Street (looking down from the top)
Note the thatched butchers shop, right

freshly-killed meat; whole carcases of pigs, lambs, rabbits and ducks; also large quarters of beef with rosettes suggesting they had been exhibited at fat stock shows; freshly dressed pigs could be seen carried down the street on the backs of the lads that worked in the slaughterhouse. One shudders to think how our modern hygiene authorities would view our meat being subject to such road-side exhibiting, all of which was so well accepted at the time.

The property owned by the "Stebbing" family permitted them to develop upon the High Road. They built and opened a dairy shop — "Meads & Blossom" — later to become a tea shop. But what was far more venturesome, by 1933 they built a small modern garage for petrol and repairs, that Stebbing's son Roy was able to build up into a successful trade, all of which now through continuous change of ownership remains to be the extensive "CROWN GARAGE".

Howgego — Wheelwright

My earliest memory of the Howgego family was in the 1920s; they lived nearby in Bull Street. It was a very old house surrounded by sheds and yard, from which he carried on a wheelwright's business, making and repairing farm carts. He also made coffins in his workshop, and conducted funerals, mainly for the poorer families. As such work seemed to dwindle, he and his son Jack, developed an interest in motor mechanics, and obtained two or three old Daimlers and De Dio Bouton cars, which attracted the interest of such fellows as Bourn and Scilitoe. They also hired them out. The front room of their house was extended to accommodate the local post office of which Mrs Howgego was the postmistress. All mail was taken to Romford and fetched by pony van. By 1923 the post office was transferred to Crow's Drapery Shop, in Crown Street, and the building was re-let for the purpose of collecting the Parish Council's rates. After which the whole yard took on

Bull Street
Showing Howgego's Cycle Shop, Wheelwright's Yard,
Small Post Office adjoining the old Bull Inn, centre

one of the first garage effects of the village. Apart from repairs they first introduced the sale of petrol from a pump which consisted of a fifty-gallon galvanised drum mounted on two wheels, that could be taken out in front to serve one or two gallons of "Red Line" petrol. The pump, possibly four feet high, with a hose attached to fill one's own can, not direct into the vehicle; most cars carried a two-gallon can, a whole "HEATH ROBINSON" affair, compared with today's self-service pumps. They also kept a few well-maintained cycles, that were for hire at sixpence per hour, and stocked such accessories as puncture outfits, tyres and inner tubes, cycle clips, lamps, and dress guards for ladies' cycles.

The family lived a simple life. Howgego's son suffered with a disability from the First World War, of which he died in 1952. The daughter, Avis, was somewhat retarded. Walter Howgego retired with all his derelict building and tools around him. They both lived to a great age, but have since passed on. In 1956 the old house was demolished and in due course the ground fell within the village redevelopment.

Townsend — Coal Merchant

The Townsends were very honest and hard-working tradesmen. Most days Alf and his brother Chris and possibly Tom Cope, could be seen unloading a coal truck in the sidings at Dagenham Railway Station. They would fill large black greasy-looking sacks to weigh 1 cwt, stack them onto their flat-bottom coal trolley, to deliver around the village.

In the 1920s, coal was priced at 2s 6d per cwt, marked up on the cart. Folk who could afford it, and had the storage space, would order special deliveries of perhaps a half or one ton. On such deliveries, to where there was no rear access, meant walking through what was the "front room" to be shot out into the coal bunker in the backyard. Customers would invariably count the sacks as they were emptied and returned to the trolley. Weights & Measures Inspectors would make spot checks to re-weigh, to make sure some unscrupulous coal man had not taken a large piece out of each bag to fill an extra one. It was a dirty job for all concerned. Most village homes depended on a coal fire, even for cooking.

There were also the odd occasions that they would use their

flat-bottom trolley to recover a deflated balloon that had come down in a field. They would return it to the station for transporting to some distant town.

With the coming of central heating, gas and electricity, plus the ever-increasing cost, the trade gradually petered out, which seemed to coincide with the Townsend's retirement age. In his younger days "Alf" had worked as a senior horseman at the local Rookery Farm.

Palmers — Drapery

Mrs Palmer had a drapery shop on the Parade in Church Street, of which included general haberdashery. There certainly was a variety of goods, from women's clothing, tablecloths, ribbons and buttons and materials. Mrs Palmer herself could have been considered a little overweight, as was her daughter Mona.

There were times when my brother and I would have to accompany my mother to visit the shop. On these occasions my mother would make sure I held her hand to avoid playing with the cottons and knocking over the cuffs and collars, precariously perched on a stand. The visit was a bore, and I tried to glean some little interest from the gossip that my mother and Mrs Palmer were able to produce. My younger brother would be perched on the end of the counter with Mona, to share some sweets, purchased from Allens Sweet Shop, next door.

Most items were priced with odd farthings, such as 6¾ d. After offering even money, she would ask if you would accept pins, as she had no farthings, to which she would pick up a pink or blue paper to tear off a row of pins. As most women did some needlework they were willingly accepted, although I was never sure who gained most from this sort of transaction. Completing a visit to Mrs Palmer's Drapery Shop, I am now sure that my mother would have gained something in excess of the purchase, for that was typical village trading.

Tom Brown — Ragman

In the 1920s, Tom Brown could be seen about the village at least once a week, sitting up in his four-wheeled cart. He had a crafty-looking face under his turned-down tweed hat, and with a ragged drooping moustache, he looked every bit the part. He would ring a brass handbell to alert his presence and call "Rag, Bottle or Bone", the later in demand for knife handles etc. (well before plastic). The sight of a possible donor, would bring him to his feet, place the offering within his own sack, which he held upon a brass spring balance. His observance would prompt him to offer a few coppers, which were usually accepted without question, for what was little more than unwanted rubbish.

His business must have spread over many years, for I have seen a picture of him using a hand-drawn coster barrow, beyond my memory of him. Threatened at being handed over to him by my mother, for misbehaving when quite young, did much to make me very suspicious of him; yet like so many such folk, he had a good side to his nature. For many Christmases he would stand outside the Vicarage Field gates with an unlimited supply of oranges that he was delighted to hand out to all the children who quickly spread the message "Old Tom Brown, was there, hurry".

West and Coe — Builders and Undertakers
Away back in 1893, Ted West and Harry Coe, were two legally-bound apprentices, to serve their master Mr George Pearcey, the village builder and undertaker. After five years together, they had completed their time, and in 1898 they formed an official partnership to carry out contract carpentry work, mainly in neighbouring Hornchurch, so not to offend their old master. They apparently worked hard and long hours to obtain sufficient capital, to commence building houses in Devonshire Road, also Harrow Drive, and very soon were invited to establish themselves by taking over their former master's business, and boldly announce to Dagenham village in 1903, that West and Coe were Builders and Undertakers.

They settled down to carry on with its simple demands. knowing their clients, and feeling quite confident to carry out the few funerals that were required. They also inherited the Parish Church's maintenance work. They were engaged to completely re-roof the nave. "The Great War" caused almost a shut down, with no men available. By 1919 when men returned, extensive work was carried out at "Woodlands" for

West and Coe, Builders and Undertakers
with The White House in the background

farmer, Mr James Parish. A large house was built opposite
Hornchurch Church, which is now the vicarage. The removal
of the church spire, and all too soon the coming of the LCC
Estate, made further demands. A new Church Hall, St.
Mary's in Grafton Road, certain alterations to Valence House
for the Council to meet. At the same time the ever-increasing
demand upon the funeral side began to take priority. About
this time the Parish Council had vacated the village fire station,
of which formed part of the families' property. This prompted
them to convert the building into the first village undertaker's
premises. It soon became established to help the new residents,

returning many funerals to their former burial ground in the London area; and so West and Coe cannot only claim to be the longest surviving business, but have continued to keep space with the town's growth.

Chas Fuller — Harness Maker
Chas Fuller's Harness Maker's Shop was in Bull Street. He lived with his widowed mother, over the shop, that formed a dual purpose, for he spent many hours seated in front of his bench, that also formed a counter for his retail trade. His harness making and repairs were in great demand, being surrounded by so many farms. The customers visiting the shop would be fascinated to watch him neatly sewing the leather straps to produce complete sets of harness, of which he was justly proud. Apart from such work he had developed a large trade in a variety of goods that were required in their time. As most folk repaired their own boots, pieces of leather, brads, rubber soles and round heels that would turn when worn down

Chas Fuller, Harness Maker, Bull Street

on one side, Nugget and Cherry Blossom boot polish, dubbing, required by farm labourers. Men would also select a leather purse from a card that hung in the window. Horsemen would purchase 1″ coloured braid, especially on May 1st, when all street traders would compete to decorate their horses' manes and tails. He also sold dog collars and muzzles, and quite often a bowl of new-laid eggs, gathered from his own backyard chickens.

With such a variety of supply he certainly entered well into the spirit of village life of his day. He also took upon himself the extra job to cycle round the village to deliver the morning post, before starting a day's work in the shop, of which I suppose gave him plenty to think about. As the farms began to disappear in the 1920s, he forsook his trade and married Gertrude Farrance, daughter of a well-known fruit grower and took over a sub post office in South-East London until he retired.

Winch — Greengrocer
Around about 1923, the "Winch" family moved into Dagenham village and took over the greengrocer's shop from the Rayment family, at the bottom of Crown Street. This was just about the time the new LCC Estate was calling out for supplies, and so it was the "Winches" who were able to put four or five horse and carts to deliver fruit and vegetables to quite a large area. Winch rented a meadow near to the "Canal" bridge to rest his horses. His large family of boys and girls all helped in his success.

One could only admire his vision that prompted him to erect a large wooden hut on a piece of spare ground at the rear of the shop. It was used to train his own boys and many other the art of boxing. In its day it became a very popular and successful club. After their parents' departure, the shop remained in the family, until with all other property in the village, it was acquired by the Borough Council for redevelopment.

Arthy's — Bakers
Everybody appeared to know of "Arthys" the bakers, that were very well-established in Crown Street. The family possibly included four boys and two girls; they lived over the

E

shop and in due time either found themselves working in the
bakehouse or the girls in the shop. The establishment included
a large well-built bakehouse and stables for their horses. As
large quantities of flour were consumed, a steam Foden
delivering it, would block the narrow street for quite a time,
something one just had to accept as justifiable, even if
inconveniencing other transport.

Mr Arthy himself was of an Edwardian appearance, with his
trimmed beard. He could be seen superintending his business,
wearing a grey tweed frock coat with matching turned down
hat. He was very particular in respect of his bakery and
dispatch, which was carried out with his eye to cleanliness and
care. The shop changed very little in my time. After viewing
the selection of bread and cakes laid out in the window, some of
which were placed on glass shelving supported by polished
brass brackets, it needed a couple of steps up into the shop, of
which on the opposite side of the spotlessly clean scrubbed pine
wood counter, were four wooden-built corn bins,
approximately two feet square. These were filled, one with
wheat, another oats, maize, and the last one was mixed; such
was in demand because most families kept chickens or rabbits.
As children we were fascinated to just let the kernels run
through our fingers, of what was mainly chicken food.

It was quite a performance to purchase a pound of biscuits,
for on a shelf behind the counter stood a selection of seven-
pound Peak Freans and Huntley & Palmer tins, with their
respected variety clearly marked. Such names as Bourbon,
Nice, Osborne, Shortcake, Custard Creams and Ginger Nuts
(all names that appear to live on). After selection, the tin would
be opened, to handle sufficient to place in a white bag on the
bright polished brass scales on the counter, to hand over. It
certainly required a little more effort if one required a mixture,
which would mean opening several tins and handling two or
three from each.

There was always a good choice of fresh oven baked loaves,
"Sandwich", "Long Tin", "Round Tin", "Cottage" and
"Hovis Brown" loaves, all priced at 2½d. Cottage loaves were
in demand, for farm labourers would enjoy their lunch from
thick slices of the bottom part with their meat or cheese, for it
seemed to keep moist. My own mother would buy "Long Tin"

to evenly slice for our tea. We would almost fight over who would get the crust, with a flavour I have never forgotten. Jam puffs in various shapes were plentiful at seven for $3\frac{1}{2}$d. They also specialised in fancy cream cakes, which after a personal selection were placed in a white card box.

One was mostly served by a member of the family, although Miss Hunt, their accountant, could be seen working in an adjoining room. Jack Ellis, was one of their most trusted and long-serving roundsmen, for many years to be seen trotting Arthy's van on his daily round. Later he carried on around the shop area with a handcart, until the business was forced to close down, due to village redevelopment. It was then we realised just how well we had been served. For they were an essential part of our village. One could walk round to the back door if an emergency arose, and be willingly served with an extra loaf. I can also recall their willingness to cook the large joints of beef in their ovens for the village Annual Old Folks' Christmas Dinner, and it would be delivered round to the nearby Methodist Hall steaming hot!

Johnny Brown — General Store
"Johnny Browns" as we knew it, was at the bottom of the street, next to Payne the butchers. Managed by himself and his brother Israel, two well-meaning bachelors that sold practically everything in the hardware line; often referred to as "Harrods Stores". Much that they were able to exhibit in the old-fashioned bay window, a glass jar was always prominent in the window with those large arrowroot biscuits that one could make a meal from, which had lost their appeal, faded almost white in the sun. Arranged around this would be flypapers, Hudson's soap powder, hearth stone block, for whitening front door steps, Brasso metal polish, black lead for the grate, emery paper, and knife powder to place on the board to clean steel knives; Sunlight soap, Lyons tea, nails, screws, bolts and padlocks; all readily available in the small cluttered shop. When one stepped down onto the concrete floor, there was little room, apart from the spot where one positioned himself to be served from a pinewood counter, so continously scrubbed that the wood grain had formed deep ridges. Within all his stock, paraffin was in continuous demand. My brother told me

of his own recollection of one particular visit, being sent down with a can for a gallon of paraffin of which he confidently placed on the counter. So particular they were, it was immediately furiously knocked off, and he was told never to do such a thing again, or he would not be welcome in the shop.

The Brothers Brown seemed like old men to us children then, and by 1922 they had had enough, and within a few years all was demolished and replaced by modern shops.

Fred Steadman — Shoe Repairer

Fred Steadman carried on a fairly busy trade of boot repairs. He was a jolly man, although his legs were severely handicapped. He spent most of his day seated on a stool in the bare front room of his cottage in Bull Street, faithfully attended by his wife and family. A visit on a cold winter's day would be made that much more welcome by the sight of an open coal fire, that was also capable of consuming most of the waste pieces of leather from his repairs.

Seated with his 'hobbing' foot in front, on the floor, his work mainly consisted of replacing worn soles and heels to heavy boots. After shaping a piece of leather, Fred would pick up a few brads, place them between his lips, from which he had developed a knack, to spit them out one at a time, with a speed to receive a rythmic strike, with a flat rasp, possibly repeating the motion a hundred times to completely secure the sole to the boot. A speedy art he had acquired over so much repetition! — Most fascinating to watch.

As children we were always welcomed to watch him work, and possibly to retain our company, he would tell us tales. The one I have never forgotten was, Bulphan Fen, was where they shoed geese, by first making them walk on tar, then on sand; so convincing, that we would repeat it. Each evening after a day seated on his stool, he could be seen making the few steps with great effort, to join his friends for a drink and chat at the Bull Inn.

Grays Co-operative Store

The Co-operative Store was half-way down Crown Street next to the bank. It was a large shop for it needed no family accommodation, being managed by a Pat Hills for many years, and supplied by their Grays depot.

Shopping at the Co-op in the 1920s is worth recalling for very few groceries were pre-packed.

The shop was set out with a counter the full length of the shop with possibly two sets of scales. A large lump of butter and margarine were placed on marble slabs with a bowl of water, two wooden pats were used to cut a piece off, and by continuous pating and shaping incorporating small particles of water, it was possible to form a presentable shape to be weighed and wrapped in greaseproof paper. A large block of cheese required a wire and toggle to cut any weight. A large jar of pickles was on hand to serve small quantities into one's own jar. Pieces of bacon piled on the counters were held up for customer selection and sliced thick or thin as preference required; also available was a large box of dates packed solid that would require chiselling off. Upon shelves at the back of the counter ample packs of CWS tea, Fry's cocoa, various CWS tinned fruit and jams. On the floor opposite would be sacks of white and brown sugar, rice and rolled oats. An assistant would pick up a piece of strong blue paper, twist it into a cone and place the approximate amount on the scales to add or subtract a little to obtain the correct weight, and finally close the cone by tucking the top over. Large blocks of wet salt were offered for brine as there was no refrigeration in those times. Large bars of Sunlight soap, loose starch and soda for the weekly wash (certainly no packets of detergents or soap powder) as most garments were of wool or cotton; easy-wash nylon was not even thought of.

When one had completed their purchase, it was reckoned up on one of the packets and entered in on the counter receipt book. You were then asked for your 'Share' number (ours was 5008), if you had forgotten or were not a shareholder, it was marked N/N (no number) and any dividend we understood was credited to a charity within the society. A small receipt of approximately two inches by one inch was handed out to keep.

In those days they appeared to trade very well with a large and varied stock, plus the dividend credited that caused a little extra excitement if it should increase a little from the previous year. In spite of all the advantages offered, there were other family grocers able to compete with them personally and endeavour to serve their customer well.

NICKNAMES

I have chosen this page to write down a few village nicknames, and although I would be guilty of using them, I would find it difficult to explain their origin. All were males and I assume possessed a similar christian name which usually fell within the common John, Edward, George, Thomas, William and Alfred. So maybe the nickname helped to define and characterise a certain fellow, for they all ended with a respectable surname:

Lob Arnold	Nobby Clark
Googie Hawkins	Brusher Smith
Tucker Winch	Jucy West
Woody Townsend	Wag Reed
Snapper Downs	Gigler Rawlinson
Knifee Bennett	Scan Tipp
Bump Arthy	Waxy Palmer
Titch Chaplin	Trowy Canham
Brumy Bush	

I am sure there are some readers who could add to my list, all of which were in daily use during 1920—30.

CHARACTERS

Mr Marino

Mr Marino and his family were Italians and moved into Dagenham in 1924. He acquired a large coster barrow that he kept in Howgego's yard. Each morning, he would most elaborately display all kinds of choice fruit, to present folk with an irresistible urge to purchase and "Eat more Fruit". Complete with scales and paper bags he would be seen pushing his barrow through the village and serving by the road side. For such performances he was continually moved on by the police, for causing an obstruction. To which he would appeal to his customers in broken English, that such was victimisation, "Because he was a foreigner".

As his family grew up to support him, he continued working very hard, and succeeded to the extent, he was able to take over a shop in the Heathway for confectionery, and subsequently set up an ice-cream trade, supplied by his own small plant, even to develop a wholesale trade. The success of such an establishment, I have little doubt, prompted him to reflect upon a village that did not readily accept him when he had nothing, for he now found himself becoming a popular man with a keen interest in local sport. In 1931 he became President of Valance Swimming Club, and gave the "Marino Cup" to be challenged each year at the gala; local press gave coverage to his generosity and public spiritedness.

The tragic death of one of his sons in 1938, who was training to be an air pilot, was killed in a motor-cycle accident, began to see the fading out of Mr Marino's outgoing personality. He

71

died in 1948, but not without leaving his mark to generously return something of what he was able to take out of the town. Another of his sons was able to carry on the business for a time.

Old Harrington

Around 1920, "Old Harrington" like most plumbers, was a little deaf. He could be seen about the village with his battered old trilby hat, ragged moustache, and steel-rimmed glasses on the end of his nose. He would carry his tools in a black Gladstone bag, and he was quite well accepted to carry out such work.

He lived with his wife, daughter and son-in-law, in a quaint corrugated iron cottage at the bottom of Crown Street by the brook. The building formed two separate dwellings. By 1923 he caused much attraction to himself by buying and bringing the first 'T Model Ford' car into the village. He certainly was the type to learn to master it, and soon was able to offer folk to hire it, for those who had the pluck to trust his driving, plus the fact that one of the back seats was mostly occupied by his wife, who would make sure you knew it was bought with her money. The whole venture proved a great success, for he accepted contracts with the doctor on his daily calls, and the villagers continued to appreciate his foresight and confidence. His equally ambitious grandson, George Suffield, built a 'Lock Up' shop in their front garden beside the road, and created quite a trade in new and second-hand cycles and accessories. It carried on, until like most village business, ceased to exist due to redevelopment.

Reverend Herbert Marshall

The Reverend Herbert Marshall came into Dagenham, during the early 1930s, from a Stratford parish, to be appointed the first Vicar of St. Georges, Rogers Road. A work he claimed to have enjoyed working among the many new families that had moved down from East London. Apart from his efforts to fill his church, he entered into many social services' committees and chaired such meetings to provide and improve the lot of folk throughout the town, much of which combined with the Borough Council's efforts to develop a social and moral structure for the new town.

He continued a very popular figure in the town until after the war in 1945; for reasons best known to himself, he took over as the Vicar of Chadwell Heath, still remaining within the Borough. By 1957, he was honoured and installed as a Canon of Chelmsford Cathedral. He continued on until 1976 when his health was failing him to retain his former vigour. It was a very proud day for him when his Borough Council had chosen to honour him as one of the very few "Freemen"; but sadly he died within a few weeks, in his 76th year, after serving his Chelmsford Diocese for fifty-three years as a priest.

His funeral service was held within his own church and was attended by a very large congregation including many civic dignitaries and representatives of a wide spectrum of the town's organizations, all gathered in grateful respect and appreciation of his unstinting service for over fifty years, contributing much to the development of the new town, both morally and socially.

Mark Sutton

Mark Sutton caught something of Baden Powell's enthusiasm for training boys to become good citizens.

Away back during the First World War, he took charge of Dagenham's first village troop, from Will Pearcey, its founder scoutmaster. It was under the control of the Wesleyan Methodist Chapel. From then on, scouting became his life involvement, with the support of his wife and family, for he had a son in the troop. He lived in Glebe Road, he had a small shed attached to his house where he kept the camping equipment. He was an outstanding character. Short and bearded always able to look the part, his bright keen eyes did much to match his keen interest in scouting for boys. He readily adjusted to the ever-increasing number of boys joining from the new LCC Estate.

His scouting life for Dagenham extended over forty years, receiving the highest awards from scouting headquarters in recognition of his outstanding service. When he died in 1955 at the great age of ninety years, he left an indelible memory to all associated with the Dagenham Scout Movement.

Mrs Prosser Evans

Doctor and Mrs Prosser Evans resided at "The Homestead" in the High Road. In the 1920s, doctors had to survive entirely upon their own merit, and in consequence were eager to establish good relations with the local inhabitants. Quite apart from the doctor's own ability to be well received, Mrs Evans was blessed with a most attractive outgoing personality and became renowned for her ability to organise many local folk that were willing to help her succeed in all she attempted to do, to help any in need. My own first memory within her grip, was as a member of "The Young Helpers' League", raising funds for Dr Barnardo's Homes. She would encourage us to display posters and sell tickets for various concerts and dances that she would promote, calling upon us for any help she would need. Incidently, I did receive and have kept, a silver thanks badge for my efforts.

Young Helpers' League in National Dress Costumes, outside the Church Hall, 1920. Photograph includes: Doris Bailey, Amy Maddock, Gladys Reader, Florrie Allen, Alf Townsend, Elsie Chandler, Grace Cooper, Leslie Richards, Pansy West, Fred Hopkins, --- Edwards, --- Vaisey, Nellie Mansfield and Mrs Prosser Evans centre

Her ability to walk through the village as such an outstanding figure, so keen and able to chat to any and all, who were more than willing to accept her friendly interest, which would mostly conclude with "You *will* be coming to my concert on Saturday in aid of Dr Barnardo's Homes — here, take a few tickets — return them if you don't sell them". And so one was drawn into the net, for it was not easy to avoid her, even if one wished to, until times changed and her more influential friends could "escape" within their cars.

As stated in another chapter, it was entirely due to her inspiration and ability to attract the help of a few ladies willing to help her that she was able to provide a clinic with the opportunity to lighten the load of mothers that needed supporting. The picture with her mothers and babies seated in a charabanc for a day out, says it all — for she had no children of her own.

There were some who felt her sense of importance was a little overpowering, but I am sure upon reflection she gave herself to those around her and retained a dignity that was exclusive to her as Mrs Prosser Evans. She found so much in common with the Reverend H. Marshall of St. Georges, Rogers Road, sharing much of his interest in a social gospel, all so necessary in a new town trying to find its way. She had to spend many years as a widow in her lovely home at Emerson Park and quietly slipped away in 1966, having reached her eighty-seventh year.

Mrs Bales
Mrs Bales was a widow, since her policeman husband died in 1910, leaving her to look after four boys and four daughters. They lived in an old converted village inn "The Rose and Crown", half-way down Crown Street, opposite Arthy's Bakers. They had a couple of meadows and stables out the back where they kept horses, cows and chickens, from which milk and eggs were always available at the front door. With such responsibility Mrs Bales developed a strong attitude to life. Three of her sons continued to live with her and set themselves up as Cartage Contractors, carting coal from the railway station to the Beam Water Pumping Station, and supplying the Local Council with horse and carts for road works, long before the Council got round to buying their own equipment. They

later took over small farms at Chadwell Heath and Blackmore.

One of my earliest memories of the 1920s, was of a small notice board, displayed outside her front door, offering seats for an outing to Epping Forest. I can recall watching the day trippers mount the 'Four in Hand' horse-drawn Breke, outside her house, to be seated high up in rows, as we now see "open top" buses. Then a few years later, she was able to offer folk seats in the newly-acquired charabanc, again seated in rows with open top, although a cover came over if it rained. They were supplied by Palmers of Oldchurch Road, Romford, who were able to advertise *"Romford Times"* along the bonnet. Day trips were now offered as far as Clacton and Maldon. Leaving her house in the morning, the occupants would throw out a few coppers to the school children in response to their call to "Chuck out your Mouldies", as they cheered them on their great adventure.

Mrs Bales remained quite a character, often seen standing by her front door in her long black dress, until she died in 1950, in her ninety-fifth year.

Dan McGregor
Dan McGregor, a real Scotsman, came into the village in the early 1920s; he soon became a familiar character, noted for his entertaining, singing and impersonating "Harry Lauder". He also made one or two broadcasts with the BBC to add to his reputation.

After a time, he was able to attract quite a few men to offer their talents to form the "Dagenham Male Voice Choir" which became very popular in raising funds for church and charities. About that time, Dagenham became quite excited, after being promised we would have our own local hospital, for which he went all out to help raise funds. Unfortunately the whole project took a different turn, when the effort was transferred to what is known as King George's Hospital, Ilford. Although Dagenham did receive a clinic attached to the hospital, built at Five Elms.

"Mac" continued with his entertaining, with an unusual amount of youthful vigour to match it, until he died in 1973, in his eighty-seventh year.

CHURCHES

Parish Church

By far the oldest and most prominent in the village is the Parish Church, of which from its outward appearance has changed very little during my time. The nave was completely reroofed in 1913, of which I was pictured at the scene, although such is beyond my memory. In June 1921 the spire (similar to that of Hornchurch) was taken down, being declared unsafe due to dry rot, and the inability to raise sufficient funds, so soon after the Great War, to repair it. It was felted over and a flagstaff erected. The original weather vane was fixed to a corner of the tower, but for some years now it has not appeared on pictures of the church.

As for the interior, several years ago, the gallery we enjoyed as young people, was used to support the pipe organ when it was removed from the chancel. In 1935 with the help of a local family's generosity, the peel of eight bells were all recast and a steel grillage was added for their support. All appeared a great asset, until the vicar had to give way to residents' complaints, living so near, all of which formed part of the Local Council's development, so near to the church. As a result, the belfry louvres were blocked up.

Up to a few years ago, all the very old church registers were kept in a chest in the vestry, and searching by appointment with the vicar was simple; now that they have all been transferred to the Chelmsford Archives, it is not so easy.

It seems a little strange, when one stops to think of the many noble men and women whose bodies lie buried beneath the chancel floor, which is frequently walked on, with little thought of all they meant to the village in their time. Some fifty years ago, a member of the Fanshaw family, asked the vicar, Revd George Jones, if he could consider to open their tomb "to clean and whiten it", the vicar and his wardens declined, not wishing to disturb anything, mainly on hygienic grounds. For many years the incumbent enjoyed the large old 17th century vicarage, with its extensive garden. Also there was a large plot adjoining, with various sheds and stables, known as the "Vicar's Hoppit". The vicar let this out to supplement his income. Beyond, and enclosed, was a large field or meadow, Glebe Land, known as the Vicarage Field. It was used for any and all outside entertainment, that, as a village we considered it was our own for all time.

When the LCC Housing Estate became established by 1931, Dagenham Urban Council were able to lay out what was to be known as Old Dagenham Park. It was then that the Church Authorities decided that their field could be made more use of, as a factory sports ground; and so it was let out on a long lease to the Union Cable Company, which allowed them to bring the whole area into good shape and build a pavilion. The church retained sufficient ground to rebuild their hall and included their right to use the field for two days each year. The recent continued development of the surrounding area, has added much to the field's value. With many years remaining on the lease, whose owners, were already concerned at the ever-increasing upkeep costs and consequently gave consideration to surrender it, to be sold for housing development; all of such transactions were the prerogative of the Chelmsford Diocesan Board, not the Local Parish Church Council, although they were informed.

Such were also the transactions with regard to the vicarage, vacated by the Revd E. Lendon around 1981; it remained a listed building of historic interest, which is let by its present owners, as a commercial investment. After much wrangling with the Borough Council, the church finally accepted an offer of a small freehold site, adjoining the churchyard, upon which the Church Authorities built a simple vicarage for the Revd D. Spatley to reside.

Kingsley Hall

I am not sure where it got its name "KINGSLEY" from, for it started in 1929, by the "Lester Sisters" who held "Tent Missions" from a caravan on ground near their present site in Parsloe's Avenue. The then densely populated area of bewildered new residents, were attracted to the social application of their Christian message, more so with the concern they showed support to the needy during the 1930 slump. They preached a social gospel and within a few years, were able to build the hall, to include a chapel for Sunday worship, also kitchens and halls to supply the needs of the people around them. The whole venture became entrusted to such an enthusiastic leader, Pastor Sidney Russell, a man completely unattached, able to give himself entirely to help others, in all sorts of ways. He continued to expand his work and enlarge his building; he took complete charge from 1932, until he died in 1988, having obtained the honour of a Mayor's Chaplain, and rewarded by the Borough Council's recognition as a "Freeman of the Borough" for his selfless, devoted religious and social services.

Salvation Army

In the very early days of the estate, the Salvation Army built a hall upon an allotted site in Dagenham Avenue. Although a little remote and isolated, it appeared to be quite well received with much to offer such a new estate. With the support of a few very devout members it continued to function through the years, although in recent years, its support dwindled down so low, as to sadly become unviable to continue. By 1990 the corps was disbanded, or transferred and the building demolished. The site was taken over by the Borough Council and a resident centre built for the elderly, which appeared a very justifiable use of the site, and quite well accepted by the surrounding residents.

St. Peter's RC

St. Peter's which started as the very first Roman Catholic Church in Dagenham, with its parish priest, Revd Fr. Holms, residing in a council house in Dagenham Avenue. They were allotted a site in Gorsebrook Road, during the mid 1920s, where they were able to erect a small permanent church, promoted by an order of American Missionaries, "Our Lady of La Salette". For many years they were supported with some very tough American priests, who were able to build up a large congregation, many of which were Irish Catholics, residing on the Ryland's Estate and working hard with the Ford Motor Company. So well the church grew in numbers, that within a few years they were able to build one of the largest seating churches in the town. The original small church still stands, adapted as their social hall, with a large presbytery built between. They have also built a convent and a girl's school, that works closely with their church.

Church of The Holy Family
The "Holy Family Church" was purpose-built during the 1930s on the corner of Oxlow Lane and Halbutt Street. It is of fine architecture and with an impressive interior. Throughout the years they have been blessed with some very devout parish priests who have been able to build up a very substantial congregation. They have also built a large social hall and have their own junior school nearby.

The Mission Hall
What was known as the Village Mission Hall was a very simple square brick building, attached to a row of cottages in Bull Street (Rainham Road). Originally built by a Mr Smith, a local baker on the corner of the street, many years before my time. It continued as an independent chapel by attracting sincere and devout Christian folk. Family names that I remember associated with the cause were a Mr Cooper, mainly responsible with the "Ives" Amos and Pithouse. It was on the edge of the footpath, that on passing, preaching and singing could be clearly heard. They would also hold magic lantern services, that did something to attract us children. After many years they reformed themselves and started the New Free Church in Charlotte Road. The old hall was demolished within the village redevelopment.

Bull Street
Left: Fred Steadman Boot Repair; Charles Fuller Harness Maker
Right: Mission Hall; West and Coe; (The White House lays back);
Howgego's; The Bull Inn

Bethal Chapel
Their simple little chapel in Vicarage Road also attracted
many of the very devout Evangelistic families, for they were
blessed with an enthusiastic leader, Pastor Webb, for many
years. His efforts were rewarding, as to require a larger
building. So different to most other churches in Dagenham. To
everybody's surprise he was personably able to persuade the
then GLC to make a site available just where he decided would
take his cause in among the people, they wished to serve.
Around the Parsloe's Avenue area. They were able to build a
much larger chapel on the main road, that has appeared to
have been a well-blessed move, as they continue, on their
prominent gifted site. Conveniently situated on one of the
town's main bus routes.

F

Heathway Central Hall

The Methodist Extension Working Committee, were allotted a site in Heathway, on a bus route. By 1925 a start was made, by the building of a quite modest little corrugated iron chapel, which was able to attract some very good Methodist families, as the "Freeman" "Horspool" and "Twyford"', to become a well-established chapel. By the early part of the 1930s with large financial help from Joseph Rank, Flour Miller, a keen Methodist, they were able to build a £25,000 Central Hall, to include a caretaker's flat. The whole project was put under the charge of the Revd Maldwin Edwards, one of their top men, with the intention to appeal to the thickly populated area so nearby. Its main purpose was to provide a large amount of social work to combine with Sunday services.

About the same time Rank's son was experimenting with religious films and cinematograph equipment, of which they were able to introduce even to the extent of providing the children with a cheap form of entertainment. The fact that they were silent cowboy films, gave the kids ample opportunity to supply the effects, and they did. Later when talky films were introduced the operator would have to frequently stop the film for the excitement to die down, to hear the words.

Times changed from cinema and concerts, with the coming of television, and as the Methodist Church could not adapt itself to discos and drinking, the social work began to dwindle and attendances fell so low, that by 1970 the large hall became a "White Elephant" to the extent regrettably it was demolished in 1974 and replaced by a small chapel and several blocks of flats erected on the site.

Old Dagenham Methodist

The original Dagenham village Wesleyan Methodist Chapel was built in Bull Street in 1788, but the chapel I knew was rebuilt on the same site in 1888 by two local builders, namely W. G. Earl and George Pearcey, being both members of the chapel. It was said that they put so much into its perfection, which nearly bankrupt them. Yet for many years Mr Earl JP, remained one of its greatest supporters, while Mr Pearcy emigrated to Canada. It certainly was a fine red brick building with Gothic shaped stained glass windows. An interior wood

Methodist Central Hall, Heathway
Demolished 1974

work of pews and pulpit in solid polished pine. It also had a
small Sunday school hall attached with toilets and a kitchen. By
1934 they found it possible to fill in a disused gravel pit at the
rear, to erect a brick built hall, to cope with the large influx of
approximately two hundred children, each Sunday afternoon
service. The whole cause continued quite well, supported by
their East Ham Circuit Authority. By 1962 a large part of their
site was required by the Borough Council for widening the
Main Road; the little original hall still remains containing the
original foundation stones, set in the inside walls. After much
bargaining over compensation and resiting the new chapel,
eventually a new simple building was erected between the
existing hall and a block of recently-built council flats and
opened in 1962, to continue the Methodist cause, on which is
as near as possible to the original site of village Methodism. In
1911, with the keen help of a few of their enthusiastic members,
were responsible to start the first village troop of Boy Scouts,
and made their premises a home for very many years.

Osborn Hall

Osborn Hall is quite a large church, built in 1931, by the Congregationalists, in the midst of Osborn Square, a thickly populated part of the estate. It started off very well, under the ministry of the Revd Graves, who was able to combine much needed social work. After a time his Scottish blood directed him to gather many interested teenage girls and share his vision to teach them to play the bagpipes. His command and care for the girls' health and morals, attracted great support from the parents. As the band progressed, the girls were trained to march and perform special Scottish dancing, also to wear the special uniform with due pride.

From the beginning, their performance was very well received locally, and they soon accepted many other engagements. In 1933 they became professional. The name of Dagenham was enhanced by their acceptance to perform at national events. When travelling by train in the early days, they would be seen walking together in full dress, most dignified, hidden by a cape.

Then in 1948 they became such a commercial proposition that they were taken over by a David Land and were able to keep up their momentum for many years, until 1968 they reverted back to their former status. The church itself like all Congregational churches became, United Reformed and continues on with Sunday worship, and using its halls for social, handicap, and other welfare demands.

*   *   *   *   *   *   *   *   *

There were several other parishes set up by the Church of England, for at the commencement of the large estate, the Bishop of Chelmsford launched an appeal which met with good response. For I believe it was Miss Wills who gave St. Albans, and a Mr Keene, St. John, and the Mothers' Union of the Diocese that provided St. Elizabeths, which was opened by their patron the Duchess of York; others were supported by various donations and Church grants, none of the parish churches have been able to claim, to have become, exceptionally successful, as yet.

VILLAGE CHURCHYARD

Although for many years now there have been no new graves in the churchyard, families' existing graves are often reopened for future burials.

The church holds a complete record of *WHO* is buried, but there has never been a complete record of just *WHERE* a person is buried. That responsibility lies entirely with the family and relatives. To erect a memorial over the grave, the parish churches seldom give any legal rights, for it is generally accepted that families have an undisturbed moral claim. Over the years it has become obvious that many of the poorer folk could not afford a permanent memorial but were able to erect wooden kerbing, that in time has decayed and since removed. For a while some families would garden the space which eventually became overgrown.

During the last war, scrap iron became so acute that the ministry sought powers to commandeer all available iron and steel, which apart from iron front fences, the iron railings were removed from many of the tombs in the churchyard and obviously never replaced.

A few years ago, possibly 1988, the Government's "Manpower Scheme", spent several weeks in the churchyard, to draw up a plan and record all decipherable inscriptions upon the permanent memorials, and were able to hand over to the vicar a very valuable document from which he can locate most family graves, providing they have a memorial stone.

As with most churchyards, in spite of continuous voluntary efforts, it appears overgrown and somewhat neglected; it also suffers an unreasonable amount of vandalism; this mainly due to children from Council flats built nearby, with very low walls to climb over. Many of the very old tombs that have stood for hundreds of years, now seem to have been unreasonably disturbed. It seems sad that such a sacred ground is neglected, and has to be acceptable as inevitable in these times, mainly through lack of funds, which by the sale of their Vicarage Field, for housing development, I felt all such financial worries were over, until I was reminded that the very considerable sum involved went straight to Chelmsford Diocesan Fund to support the poorer churches with vicar's stipends and residences, by virtue of a policy adopted some few years previous, to take charge of ''Vicars' Livings'' including all property they had previously held.

It seems so sad, that during the village redevelopment the church area has been so disturbed and unreasonably disregarded, and now has had to part with the one financial opportunity that could have brought the whole church area to compare with that of Barking and Hornchurch. My personal appeal to the Diocesan office met with little response, apart from reminding me that they were acting within their legal position and that it was the Local Church Council's responsibility to find funds to maintain the churchyard of which appears a practical impossibility without some extra help.

CINEMAS

Within the space of sixty years, four cinemas have been built in Dagenham. In their time they were very well accepted and supported. Now with the introduction of television, two have completely disappeared and been replaced by shopping parades, and of the two remaining, one is converted into a bowling alley and the other of which the shell is used by a DIY store.

It was in the late 1920s that the Kay brothers built Dagenham's first cinema — "The Grange" — a fairly modest building compared with others that followed. It was built on the corner of Heathway and Gorsebrook Road and proudly operated black and white silent films, which necessitated a local pianist (Mrs Groves) to sit in front of the screen and bang away at the piano, to support the film's required effects.

Seating was offered at 6d, 9d, 1s and 1/6d for the back row, and beyond that for a set amount, one could avail themselves of a "Private Box" to completely seclude themselves or invite a small party of friends to share. All appeared very local, that knowing the usherettes a good seat was assured irrespective of cost. It was something entirely new and exciting. When talking films were introduced they made a few adjustments and greatly revived their support, but all very soon "The Mayfair" was built on the corner of Whalebone Lane and Wood Lane, a much larger cinema with very modern decor, that it was able to attract a full house for many years; sadly it is now a parade of shops. Quickly to follow was the "Princess" built on the corner of Ballards Road and New Road, which also boasted the very

Grange Cinema, corner of Heathway and Goresbrook Road
Demolished for shopping parade

Heathway Cinema, north side of the Bridge
Now reconstructed as a retail store

latest of cinema decor, complete with an illuminated 'rise and fall' organ. It was designed without a gallery, one long rise from front to back; again attracting a large support from the Rylands Estate, within the Ford factory area. As with the others, attendance began to dwindle, and it eventually gave way to a complete change of use as it was converted into a "Bowling Alley". The last to be built was "The Heathway", right in the centre and directly opposite the District Line Station, certainly destined to succeed. Eventually it became Dagenham's most popular cinema, until times changed, attendance dwindled, to the effect that the owners intimated the possible closure of Dagenham's last cinema. This almost caused a public outcry, in a bid to save it. Alas, after standing empty for a time, it was eventually taken over by a DIY store, who were able to adapt the shell for a large retail outlet.

That was the end of the exciting era of Dagenham's cinemas.

TRAGEDIES

One of the greatest tragedies to hit the village in my time, was the loss of three small children all under five years old. They were playing with matches in a garden shed which was filled with combustible rubbish for Guy Fawkes night. The three were from separate families, the "Watneys" the "Letton" and the "Knight" family. All living close to each other, near to the vicarage. Despite every effort to save them all three died together in the fire.

It was in 1926 and the new LCC Estate was becoming well established to feel part of Dagenham, although the village remained very much separated. The sympathy shown by the new residents did something to unite the two communities. The funeral was attended by so many saddened folk, who watched the three small white coffins carried from their homes, with their families following to attend a service in the Parish Church, after which they were all laid together in a special grave which had been prepared at the side of the main path. With such generous contributions received, a fitting memorial of three small white marble crosses with each appropriately inscribed, were erected over the grave, of which sadly has recently suffered vandalism. As with many other crosses for some strange reason.

Duncan
Another tragedy that befell the village in 1965 was the murder of a little eight-year-old girl "Cathy Duncan", who lived with her parents on the West Ham Estate. The report that she was

missing, immediately set up fears for her safety, with the faint hope that she may have strayed out onto the open waste ground, or even fallen into the nearby river. Anxious days continued to pass without any trace. The police, with the help of neighbours and even a Scout Troop, spent many hours searching, and imploring folk to look again in their garden sheds; all became so frustrating without any success. Local newspapers gave much coverage on behalf of the bewildered family. Then after two weeks, the news that her little body had been found hidden in a drawer in the bedroom of a neighbour, brought a sad sense of relief.

A youth was charged with her murder. He stated that Cathy had continually annoyed him. As could well be expected sympathy poured in from neighbours and friends. To support the parents, a fund was set up, to give some opportunity to share the sad loss.

The funeral attended by so many people was conducted by the vicar, Reverend E. Patterson, who arranged a befitting service; after which the small white velvet-covered coffin was placed in a grave near to the church. From funds so generously offered a suitable memorial was erected over the grave.

SWIMMING POOLS

As a child, Dagenham had no swimming pool. My earliest recollection was a visit to Romford's Mawney Road indoor baths, which was quite an effort, for there were no buses in those days. A visit to Romford meant by train to Upminster, then change back to Romford. However, what was nearly as quick and a lot cheaper, was to walk across the footpaths.

Being quite young in 1924, I recall on my very first visit, the noise and excitement of the packed baths, did much to put me off a return visit, until quite a few years later. By 1931 our own Local Council had taken over and laid out Valence Park to include an outdoor swimming pool. Now twenty years old myself, I joined with many others to enjoy all it had to offer. It would open at 6.30 a.m. in the summer months for a dip before starting a day's work, which at times meant jumping over the gates, then greet the late-arriving pool attendant from the pool. A swimming club was formed, which provided an annual gala to compete in.

On the occasion of double summer-time, 1940 I recall, the pool was floodlit to enjoy until 10.00 p.m. It all appeared so relaxing, and certainly no vandalism that I can recall. By 1939 the Council were able to provide a really super outdoor pool within the Leys, to include a social hall. The pool was designed to comply with national competition standards and was surrounded by a wide grass verge. Parents would enjoy lazing around while the children were safely enjoying themselves. Refreshments were available. A succession of poor summers, which did not claim anywhere near maximum attendance,

DAGENHAM SWIMMING CLUB

AFFILIATED TO S.C.A.S.A., R.L.S.S., E.C.S. & W.P.A.

President : S. MARINO, Esq.

ANNUAL

GALA

Under A.S.A. Laws

AT

Valence Park Swimming Bath

ON

Thursday, August 12th, 1937

Doors Open to Ticket Holders 7 p.m.
Commence 7.30 p.m.

Hon. Secretary :
W. D. THACKRAY,
57, Philip Avenue,
Rush Green.

Hon. Treasurer :
J. WHITE,
24, Lindisfarne Rd.,
Dagenham.

PROGRAMME PRICE - - - - 2d.

THE HEATH PRESS, BEACONTREE HEATH, DAGENHAM

Valence Park Swimming Bath, Annual Gala Programme, 1937

Leys Swimming Pool (looking north)
Note the high diving facilities

caused the Council to realise that Leys Pool was losing its former attraction, and so without hardly realising it, the Leys Pool completely disappeared. Almost at this time the Council had planned a modern indoor pool, that would be the answer to all-year round entertainment, whatever the weather.

It was in 1972, that the new pool opened to the public, at Becontree Heath, a more central part of the Borough. It included a small training pool and a gallery for seating spectators at competitions and galas. All started off quite well, but it was not too long before it experienced closure due to refixing loose tiles in the pool area. As this reoccurred, the local folk were suggesting that the "Old Heath Gypsies" had put a curse on the pool for it certainly has not enjoyed a good record of continuous activity.

Nevertheless, it is Dagenham's only enclosed public swimming pool, and appears to be a worthwhile expenditure.

STREET SALE OF ICE CREAM

Through Sixty Years

Our first village introduction of ice cream was away back in the early 1920s, with the arrival of what we knew as the Hokey Pokey Van; a small pony and open-sided van, with four corner twisted brass poles, supporting a striped coloured canvas roof. A little Italian-looking man would stand in it, not far off ground level. On a hot afternoon, he would position himself outside "The Bull Inn", having journeying down from Barking or East Ham. He never had to shout his presence, for it was attractive enough to bring children, who had been lucky enough to have been given the few coppers, to obtain such a rare opportunity. The little man would dip his wooden spoon into the canister floating within a large pail of ice lumps, on the floor in front of him. Upon his little brass gadget he placed a wafer from a box at his side, spreading the watery custard substance evenly over, pop another wafer biscuit on top, then hand it over to the eager customer, snatching the twopence and tossing it into a tray; rapidly pick up a cornet biscuit, to pile up sufficient on top, to accept one penny. When he was able to satisfy his little crowds that had gathered, he trotted his pony to another pitch, to find more children eager to obtain such a treat.

Hokey Pokey Ice Cream Van, 1920

95

By the mid 1930s street sales took a new scene, for the Walls' Company had introduced a fleet of box tricycles; they were painted dark blue, and apart from their name in white writing, they carried the slogan "Stop me and buy one", which became very popular in most districts. Within the box they could produce a limited variation of wrapped ice cream, of a much more creamy and acceptable package; this was produced from a chest of dry ice, from which a vapour could be seen when it was opened. The whole venture appeared to fade out with the outbreak of the war.

Walls' 'Stop Me and Buy One', 1930s

Sometime after the war had ended, and rationing had gone back to normal trading, brightly-painted, motorised vans appeared around the street, large enough to produce a greater variation of wrapped ices, apart from supplying many other kinds of confectionery. They are known as "Mr Whippy" and trading in such comfort, can be seen in all weathers, and well into the evening. They would acquaint their presence with a succession of electric recorded bells, which after a time became restricted, as an annoyance. The attraction to excited children in the street warranted a permanent warning on the rear of the vehicle "Mind that Child". They would also contract with a fête, to take up a position, for which they would pay for their static pitch.

Mr Whippy Ice Cream (Post War)